P9-CRH-363

THE SERVANT OF THE WORD

THE SERVANT
OF THE WORD

by

HERBERT H. FARMER,
D.D.

NEW YORK
CHARLES SCRIBNER'S SONS
1942

PREFACE FOR AMERICAN EDITION

I am indebted to Messrs. Scribner for giving me the opportunity to write a special preface to the American edition of these chapters on preaching and its relation to the Church's task to-day. For such a preface, whatever it may convey to any who read it, is certainly to me something like a note to old friends—if I may assume that some at least of those, both in the ministry and out of it, who honoured me with their friendship during the four years I was teaching in Hartford, Connecticut, will do me the further honour of sparing an hour or two for these pages.

I say "both in the ministry and out of it" because there lies behind the book, as indeed is explicitly stated at one or two places in it, the conviction that preaching is emphatically not the exclusive responsibility of the preacher alone. To effective preaching the hearer contributes, if not as much as the preacher, then certainly much more than he usually realises; but to understand this, it is necessary rightly to interpret the word "effective," and in particular to understand why it is important to use the word "effective" and not the word "good."

"Good" preaching may mean nothing more than that it is interesting to listen to, conforms to certain generally accepted classical standards, has certain graces and unities of style and design—qualities by no means to be despised. But "effective" preaching can only mean effective in the sense of doing God's work, and this it may assuredly do even if the qualities mentioned in the last sentence are not conspicuously present, *provided both preacher and hearer clearly and deeply understand what is supposed to be happening when preaching is taking place and solemnly acknowledge their responsibility in and for it.* "Take heed therefore how ye hear" might well be an appropriate motto to be carved upon a pulpit, not for the preacher to see, lest he be tempted to shift the responsibility too much from his own shoulders, but for his hearers, lest they be tempted to shift it too much from theirs.

It is hoped, therefore, that these chapters, though addressed primarily to ministers and those training for the ministry—as were the Warrack lectures on which they are based—may not lack a wider interest and appeal. It is hoped that if they have any value at all, they may do something to enable both those who preach and those who listen to play their proper part in the dual responsibility.

Perhaps also they may help to quicken the sense of the Church's solemn and distinctive task in this present time. Of the need for such quickening it would be superfluous to speak, and indeed in a measure impertinent; for even to suggest that the Churches either in Great Britain, or in America, or in any part of the world, are not already becoming humbly aware, amidst the dread events of these days, of the need for any such quickening would surely be to express an ultimate unbelief in them and in the Holy Spirit.

H. H. FARMER.

Cambridge, England.
June, 1942.

CONTENTS

I

THE REDISCOVERY OF PREACHING

IF one were asked to indicate in the briefest possible way the most central and distinctive trends in contemporary Christian theology, one would be tempted to answer " the rediscovery of the significance of preaching ". But one would need to insist at once, in order not to be misunderstood, that the answer be interpreted strictly in terms of the question. It would not claim to be more than the briefest possible statement we can think of in reply, an epitomising statement, one indicating, that is to say, a focal point wherein a number of different lines of thought meet rather than of itself conveying much information. And it would not have in mind more than " trends " or " tendencies ", to be discerned and felt through a number of coincidental impressions rather than to be substantiated by reference to explicit statements. And, finally, one would have to insist that such tendencies are tendencies of Christian *theology*. They have not yet taken possession in any marked degree of the mind of the man in the pew, nor, of course, in any degree whatever of the mind of

the man who is never in the pew at all.   There is
certainly no general rediscovery of the significance of preaching as yet, or even signs of it.
What we have in mind is at the moment being
wrought out in the reflection of those whose
business it is to reflect on the " deep things of
God " as given in the Christian revelation—the
theologians and, as I hope, the ministers of whom
it was truly said by Herrmann long ago that their
most distinctive function (for it is one which
no one else in the Christian community can
discharge) is to produce, preserve, and utilise a
sound theology.

There are, to be sure, other reasons than
specifically theological ones which in these days
might well lead to a rediscovery of, or re-emphasis
upon, the significance of preaching.

Thus there is the realisation to which the contemporary situation has assuredly in some
measure brought us all, that what men believe
about God and about themselves is of the utmost
importance, not only to their individual life, but
also to their national life as well.   It is plainly
quite critical for the future of the world that the
Christian way of looking at things should be
preached and taught with new devotion and
power by those who are called to do so.   And if
it be true in any sense at all, as I think it is true,

that this country of ours still has in large measure among the main springs of its life a Christian way of looking at things, despite all the evil that is in it, then that affords a still stronger reason for us to realise afresh the high significance of our calling as preachers. It is possible that in the providence of God this country is being challenged to play a special part in the crisis of the modern age. Certainly nothing could be of greater significance to the world than a Britain the soil of whose common life, if I may so put it, is no longer growing thin, stony and sour with unbelief, but rather is being penetrated anew with the salts of a Christian understanding of God and man. By the same argument nothing could be of greater importance than the work of the trained and accredited preachers and teachers of the Christian Church.

Then there is the evidence which has but recently been given us of the actual effectiveness of preaching even when seen on the vast background of world events. If it is well to think of what the preaching and teaching ministry might yet achieve, it is equally important to realise what it has in fact achieved already. Today, as the œcumenical conferences, especially the Madras Conference, brought home to us with irresistible force, the Christian Church stands as

the only truly international and dynamically
alive society in the midst of a humanity falling
to pieces around us.   That national divisions,
frightfully accentuated by war, cut deeply into
the Church's life is tragic indeed, but no one
present at the Madras meeting could doubt that
the underlying unity is there, is indestructible,
and now comprehends the whole circle of the
globe.   And how has this come about ?   It is in
large measure the direct result of the preaching
of the gospel.   Every representative at Madras
of the young churches of the Orient was a living
witness to the effectiveness of preaching.   When
the Christian Church thus takes on a dimension
commensurate with the world itself, everything
within it is magnified accordingly, including the
activity of preaching.   It is well to remind ourselves when we stand before a congregation to
preach that we are there as representatives
of the universal, supra-national church—no
longer merely a dream and a hope, but in
considerable measure, even amidst the divisions
of war, a living fact.   But when it is realised that
preaching, under God, brought that church into
being, then the significance of what we do is
enhanced still more.

Again, there is the fact that this age has come
to realise in a new way a terrible potency in

speech. For many centuries the Christian Church in this and in other western lands was in a most privileged position, one involving a stewardship of which it might well dread to be called upon of God to give an account. It had an agent, a full-time, paid agent, in every village in the land. It had access to people's minds through their ears when, because of illiteracy, every other channel was closed. The coming of universal education, and with it the power to read, exposed the masses of the people to new and potent influences in books and in the daily press, but the clergyman and minister still had a virtual monopoly of the ear, his only serious rival being the teacher during the short school years. Today, with the advent of the radio, that privileged position has gone. It has been given in an enhanced form to others. Those who direct broadcasting have an agent, not in every village only, but in every parlour in the land. In the broad sense of propaganda, the ether is full of preaching today. Indeed, the Ministry of Information has itself so rediscovered the significance of preaching that it has even sought to provide clergy and ministers with their Sunday sermons. Amidst all this babel of voices brought into every living-room by the mere turning of a knob, a man might well say with new meaning, " Woe is me if I preach not, as opportunity is given me, the gospel of our Lord Jesus Christ ! "

We are not, however, now interested in these matters, important though they be. What we have in mind is, as has been said, the rediscovery of the significance of preaching as summing up some of the most distinctive trends of contemporary Christian thought. What do we mean by this ? We mean, in general, that we are coming to see through a number of converging lines of thought that the activity of preaching is not merely a means for conveying the content of the Christian faith, but is in a real sense *bound up with that content itself*. The means and the content, the preaching and the message, are indissolubly one and cannot be separated from one another. The activity of preaching is to the faith as blossom is to the plant : it is part of it, gathers into itself all its vital forces, all its life history, all that makes it its specific and distinctive self, sums it all up and reveals it in a potent recreativeness. Preaching and message are one organic whole as a man's body and spirit are one organic whole— even though we do find it convenient to think of the one mainly as the instrument and vehicle of the other.

To say this is, no doubt, to use the word preaching in a quite special sense, in a distinctively Christian sense. But that is precisely what we intend to do. Christian preaching, rightly understood, is *sui generis*, because the Christian faith, with which it is organically one, is *sui generis*. It cannot be understood according to general principles governing propaganda. It is an incommensurable, because the Christian faith is, in its heart and essence, an incommensurable. It is exactly this that we are realising afresh today through a number of convergent lines of thought.

The point may be illustrated by reference to some paragraphs in Prof. W. E. Hocking's latest book, *Living Religions and a World Faith*. It is a book, it is quite superfluous to say, full of rich things, but, in my judgment, it suffers from one fatal defect namely, that it does not grasp the unique essence of the Christian faith. It fails in this, I suspect, because the author is not as thoroughly versed in the best Christian theology of recent years as he is in philosophy and in the comparative study of religions. One place where this failure reveals itself is in some paragraphs on preaching.[1] Prof. Hocking sees in the activity of preaching a characteristic of all living religion. It is perhaps open to question whether it is quite so universally characteristic as he suggests, but,

[1] Pp. 37f.

however that may be, it is certain that it is not characteristic of other religions in the same sense in which it is characteristic of Christianity.

In other religions the activity of preaching can be fully understood in terms of motives and impulses which, though they may receive reinforcement from the religious experience, can operate in spheres which are not specifically religious. In Christianity, on the other hand, it can only be understood in terms of the unique content of the Christian faith itself. General psychological principles do not carry you to its heart and essence at all. Prof. Hocking himself explains what he calls the " strange activity of preaching " by principles which make it cease entirely to be strange. He relates it to the need of passion to express itself in action : it can only live " by giving itself away " ; to the compassion for others which in fine natures takes on an accent of duty ; to the fear that enlightenment, in so far as it is not shared, may separate the seer from his fellows ; to the need for community— and so on. There is nothing strange about these motives, and so far as they are adequate as an explanation of the strange activity of preaching, it ceases to be strange. But I venture to think that so far as Christianity is concerned these paragraphs omit the heart of the matter. For us preaching is, and must remain, a *strange* activity ; its strangeness is irreducible, for it is part of the strangeness, the uniqueness of the Christian faith itself.

Let me now illustrate by one or two examples the statement that we are rediscovering the indissoluble oneness of preaching and the Christian faith.

The obvious example is the teaching of Barth, for whom the whole task of Christian theology starts from, and centres in, the activity of proclamation, under which he includes preaching and the sacraments, with, I think, the main emphasis on preaching.[1] Dogmatics is the Church reflecting upon, testing itself in respect of, its task of proclamation. It is the Church seeking to make clear to itself what its message is. But I do not wish to speak here of particular thinkers, except as examples of what has now become a general trend uniting schools of thought which in other respects differ greatly from one another. Barth's strong emphasis on preaching is perhaps the outstanding example of a new realisation—which was bound to come sooner or later, for it had never been really lost from the devotional life of the Church—of the sheerly objective, historical, underived givenness, which

[1] *The Doctrine of the Word of God* (Eng. Tr.), Chap. I.

the Christian revelation claims for itself. It claims to rest on something unique, decisive, critical which God Himself did " for us men and for our salvation ". Its fundamental dogma, in which all other dogmas are implicitly contained, is that in Jesus Christ God came into human history, took flesh and dwelt amongst us, in a revelation of Himself, which is unique, final, completely adequate, wholly indispensable for man's salvation. It all begins in an Event, or rather The Event, God's Event. The essential content of Christianity therefore is not something which men, even of superlative intellectual and spiritual power, could ever discover by the exercise of their own powers. For reflection can never establish the actuality of a historical event. The most it can establish is the possibility of an event, or at most, if the event have congeners and parallels, its probability. An event can only establish itself—by happening, by being given. And it can only become generally known by being borne witness to, by being proclaimed, by the story being told. The more unparalleled it is, the more, obviously, this is so.

From the beginning, then, Christianity, being concerned with The Event which by definition has no parallel, God being agent in it as He is not in other happenings, was committed to preaching, to proclamation. Whoso said Christianity, said preaching. There was no choice between that and absolutely ceasing to be, with not the least chance of ever occurring again. It is theoretically conceivable that all the sacred books of Hinduism, and every Hindu, might be utterly destroyed, and yet substantially the same religion reappear. It is not very likely ; but it is not a self-contradictory idea. Indeed it would fit harmoniously into the Hindu scheme of thought to suppose that if Hinduism vanished today it would reappear tomorrow, fifty years, a thousand years hence. But were all Christian records and all Christians extirpated, Christianity could not recur again. In its recurrence without a preacher, without a witness, it would flatly contradict all that it had always claimed to be. To put it paradoxically, in happening again it would show that it had never, according to its own definition of itself, happened at all.

But, further, along with this emphasis on the objective, historic, unrepeatable Event there has gone in contemporary theology a new realisation of the significance of the Church as itself part of the Event, part of the divine, saving activity in history. The Event to which the Church bears witness is not receding farther and farther into the distant past, but is still going on, and *the*

Church itself is part of its ongoing. Such a thought is certainly not new ; it is implicit in the experience and the doctrine of the Risen Christ, the Holy Spirit and the Sacraments. But it is being brought home to us afresh and from a new angle today in connexion with a rediscovery of the significance of the eschatological element in the Christian outlook.

I am thinking particularly of the view which Prof. Dodd has set forth so persuasively in this country on the basis of the profoundest New Testament scholarship and research, and which is destined, I believe, to become more and more deeply part of the self-consciousness of Christians today, the view he has taught us to associate with the phrase " realised eschatology ". God's saving act into the darkness and evil of human history has already taken place in the coming of Jesus Christ, but it is not yet the completed act. It is still going on, and it will be finally wrought out in that consummating event which, in God's good time, will both close and fulfil the long, and apparently meaningless, travail of the years. The kingdom is already in our midst, but it is not here in its fulness. The Event is the eschatological event, the dénouement of history, already begun. To use Heim's image, in the coming of Christ the lightning has flashed, but the thunder of God's final victory is yet to sound ; yet lightning and thunder are one event. Now into this stream—to change the metaphor—of God's *saving* activity in history (we emphasize the word " saving ", for it is by no means denied that God is active in other things as well) the Church is taken up. It is already part of it, one with it. It is already within the eschatological event which has begun in Christ. Dodd and Otto have made clear that all this is not a merely modern idea, but is a recovery of New Testament thought and experience, nay, a recovery of something deep and central in the mind of the Master Himself. It only appears modern because it has been for so long lost sight of, and because, in the good providence of God, it has been recovered at a time when we modern folk greatly need its comfort and challenge.

But our interest is in preaching. It is not difficult to see how deeply this whole line of thought affects our understanding of the significance of preaching. Bearing witness to the unique, saving activity of God in Christ is now seen not as merely an adjunct, even an indispensable adjunct to, but as indispensably part of, the saving activity itself. It is carried by it, and itself carries it. The motives for preaching, therefore, which Professor Hocking mentions in

the passage already referred to, though they may
be present in the Christian preacher, do not,
as we have said, touch the heart of the matter.
It is not the necessities of *our* nature, even our
redeemed nature, which are being satisfied in the
activity of preaching, but, if we may so put it,
the necessities of God in the prosecution of His
own sovereign purpose. This finds expression in
the Church's conviction that it has received a
direct, divine *commission* to preach the gospel.
This commission is not just a sense of inner
compulsion such as might spring up in the heart
of any generous nature, but is part of the original
givenness of Christ Himself. It is the incarnate
Lord's own command that we should go and
preach the gospel of the Kingdom. Witnessing
to the event was indeed part of the event from
the very beginning. The first thing that is said
of Jesus is that He " came *preaching* the good news
of the Kingdom of God ".

It is by no means suggested that preaching is
the only activity of the Church which finds place
in " saving history "—far from it. Works of
compassion, for example, such as must surely
flow from any sharing in the mind and activity
of Christ (for they too were part of the original
event) also find place in it. Yet preaching, in one
form or another, is obviously the basic, the pivotal

thing, without which other activities have little power, and that only in a very indirect and uncertain way, to serve the saving, divine purpose which has entered history in Christ. It is not without significance that the Gospel record of Christ's commission to His disciples puts preaching first and then the healing of the sick. A work of compassion even of the most devoted and sacrificial kind tells nothing *per se* about the gospel of the kingdom of God. It only begins to speak of that when it is associated with, and interpreted by, the preaching of the gospel. For this reason it is possible in some measure to sympathise with the disquietude which some have sometimes expressed at what they regard as the undue absorption of Christian missions in medical and educational work to the exclusion of the preaching of the gospel, and even with those who would render no medical service in a mission hospital save on the general condition that the patient listen to a gospel address. The insistence that you have not fulfilled your distinctive Christian task, taken your appointed place in " saving history " merely by healing, even though you have been led to engage in such work by your knowledge of Christ, is entirely right. What is wrong is the narrow and even wooden way in which it is sometimes sought to apply this principle.   That the prime task is to preach the gospel does not absolve from the necessity to use tact and wisdom as to time, method and place. There is a time to keep silence as well as a time to speak.   Furthermore it is a fact, as we shall later maintain,[1] that if preaching is not accompanied by some participation in men's personal situations and needs, it loses much of its power to convince. The two types of activity should be held firmly together, as they are in the gospels.   It is a perfect illustration of the principle " these ought ye to have done, and not to leave the other undone ".

We have said nothing up to this point as to why the saving event should be borne witness to in preaching.   We have said that unless it is proclaimed nobody can know about it ;   it is not to be reached by reflexion.   We have said that the preaching of it is part of the divine saving activity itself.   But why should anybody need to know about it ?   Why should preaching be part of the divine saving activity itself ?

Perhaps such questions sound superfluous. Of course, we say, people ought to be told about these things ;   it is self-evident.   But they are not superfluous.   For, in the first place, it is quite conceivable that God might act savingly

[1] See pp. 93 f.

towards men in such wise that no knowledge on their part of what He had done, or was doing, was necessary at all. Indeed such an idea has not infrequently intruded itself into Christian thought. The notion of some of the Greek Fathers that God's saving work in Christ consists in the infusion of the eternal divine life into the corrupt and mortal body of humanity suffers from the defect, among others, that it is difficult to see on that basis why anybody should need to know about it in order to benefit from it. A similar impersonalism has frequently revealed itself in doctrines of the sacraments and of saving grace. It is noteworthy that certain types of sacramentarian theology have always been associated with a tendency to minimise the place of preaching. And in the second place, if you say that it is obvious that people ought to be told about these things, I reply that merely to tell people about these things is not necessarily preaching. To raise the question why the saving event should be preached is, indeed, to raise the question what preaching, as distinct from other forms of public utterance, essentially is.

And so there comes into view another strong trend of contemporary Christian thought, one which will form the basis of much that I want to say later in these lectures. I mean that whole

c

line of thought which emphasises the quite *sui generis* nature of persons and their relationship to one another, and which received not its first but perhaps its most original expression in Buber's now well-known little book " I and Thou." I regard this as the most important contribution that has been given to us of recent years towards the reflective grasp of our faith. It has already entered deeply into the theological thought of our time, and is, I believe, destined to enter still more deeply. The so-called dialectic theologians are making full use of this line of thought, notably Brunner, but it is by no means a monopoly of theirs. Heim's work in this sphere is especially valuable.[1]

Clearly it is not possible or desirable here to attempt any complete résumé of these trends of thought. It is enough to hint at their relation to our main interest of preaching. If we are to see the reason why preaching is essential to the saving purpose of God, is part of the divine saving activity itself, we must set it in the context of this whole world of the personal and of the facts and laws by which it is constituted. Only by under-standing and remembering these facts and laws shall we be saved constantly recurring doubts

[1] *E.g.* in *God Transcendent* (Nisbet : Eng. Tr. of *Glaube und Denken*) *passim.*

whether preaching is as important as the time we spend on it would make it appear to be, as well as from making grievous mistakes. This will be further developed in a later chapter.[1] At the moment it is enough to state the central truth. It is this, that the necessity of preaching resides in the fact that when God saves a man through Christ He insists on a living, personal encounter with him here and now in the sphere of present personal relationships. Preaching is that divine, saving activity in history, which began two thousand years ago in the advent of Christ and in His personal relationships with men and women, and has continued throughout the ages in the sphere of redeemed personal relationships (which is the true Church), now focussing on me, confronting me, as a person indissolubly bound up with other persons at this present time. This focussing on me is not apart from what has gone before, nor can it be, for it is part of the continuous purpose throughout the years which began in Christ ; hence preaching is telling me something. But it is not merely *telling* me something. It is God actively probing me, challenging my will, calling on me for decision, offering me His succour, through the only medium which the nature of His purpose permits Him to use,

---

[1] See pp. 56 f.

the medium of a personal relationship. It is as though, to adapt the Apostle's words, " God did beseech me by you ". It is God's " I—thou " relationship with me carried on your " I—thou " relationship with me, both together coming out of the heart of His saving purpose which is moving on through history to its consummation in His kingdom.

Herein, I would emphasise, the distinctive nature of preaching appears. It is derived from the distinctive nature of the Christian faith. Herein also appears the reason why preaching is sometimes called, in a broad sense, a *sacrament*. For while preaching is the preacher's activity, is the preacher saying something, yet it is only distinctively preaching in so far as it is uttered and listened to in the faith, however baffling the thought may be, that it is God's activity, that it is God encountering human souls in what may at any moment prove to be the supreme crisis of their life. A sermon is not an essay in which you give utterance to your views and impressions of life, though it could hardly fail to contain in some measure your views and impressions of life. It is not a theological lecture, though it will contain theology, and the sounder the theology the better. It is not a discussion of political and social and international matters, though I for one would wish to lay down no rigid law excluding such topics. It is not instruction in Christian morals, though that will surely not be absent. It is God's great activity of redemption in history, in the world of persons, focussing itself in challenge and succour on " these persons here present ", who listen to your words and look into your eyes ; nay, it is that activity focussing on you, the preacher, also, for no man has truly preached who has not tremblingly felt the sermon penetrating his own soul also. Comments and impressions of life, theology, challenges and rebukes on social questions, moral instruction, anything in fact of *truth* that might conceivably be given to the best and humblest reflexion of a serious Christian mind, these all become specifically *preaching* precisely as they are informed by this sense that here and now God's saving activity in the world in Christ once again encounters the souls of men.

I would not therefore want in practice to press the distinction between preaching and instruction, *kerugma* and *didache*, too far. Barth I think tends to do so. The distinction is valuable in so far as it reminds us once again of the specific differentia of preaching, and brings into view again the distinctive content of the Christian faith. But if it be used in such wise as to exclude from the sermon what may be called in a broad sense instructional matter then it is misleading ; it unduly narrows the content of preaching. Everything depends on what the containing context, and what the focal point, of the sermon are. If the context is always God's saving activity through history in Christ, and if the focus is the encounter of that saving activity with those who listen, then nothing that does not fog that context or blur that focus need be excluded. It was said of a certain theological professor in my hearing, by one of his students, that to hear any one of his lectures, profound and technically learned as they were, was like listening to a powerful sermon, or even at times being present at a communion service. That was high praise. I am not suggesting that a sermon could ever with profit become a theological lecture, but that even a theological lecture in the right hands can become a sermon does at least illustrate my point. Similarly I have heard Charles Gore or George Lansbury speak on social questions in a way that made the whole utterance a preaching of the Word. Everything depends on carrying with you a sense of the living, saving, present activity of God in Christ.

These thoughts are both enheartening and

solemnising. That preaching is sacramental, that God uses it as a means of His saving approach to the souls of men and women, that it pleases God " through the foolishness of preaching to save them that believe," entitles us to go on with our task with a confidence which no purely human estimate of our powers could ever even begin to justify. But it is also a very solemnising thought. If what has been said is true at all, the preacher is one upon whom the saving strategy of God in Christ, in relation both to the individual and even to universal history, may at any moment turn, and that remains a heavy responsibility, no matter how confident we may be that the effectiveness of our preaching, if it has any, is entirely of God and not of ourselves. God may indeed use the foolishness of preaching, but we are under obligation to see that it is not more foolish than it need be. For indeed, a sermon which is more foolish than it need be, which has not our uttermost best in it, which is not written and prepared with a responsible sense of its part in the saving purpose of the Most High, is not preaching, but merely the routine fulfilment of a professional task. Not for it is the promise, though I would not say that God may not use even it as a sort of uncovenanted mercy.

A further word on this solemn responsibility

of preaching, a responsibility the full weight of which can only be felt when preaching is seen, as we have tried to see it, in the context of the whole Christian revelation, may perhaps be not out of place. I find it hard to avoid the judgment, though it is one which in the nature of the case I cannot substantiate, that the preaching in our churches is often much more foolish, much less effective than it need be, because the preacher does not really give of his uttermost best to it. He does not, in fact, work hard enough at the task ; he does not work with that maximum of concentrated purpose which would assuredly result from the perception that in his preaching God may be seeking an encounter with men and women of an unspeakably critical kind, that in it the whole historic saving purpose of God is seeking temporarily to focus itself. It is only given to very few to be a F. W. Robertson or a C. H. Spurgeon, and no effort can enhance our powers beyond their appointed limits. Yet only effort, and even drudgery, can prevent them from falling consistently below their appointed limits, and that effort, if our understanding of the significance of preaching be not false, it is almost blasphemy to withhold.

In particular, it is, I think, a capital error, which many make, to suppose that when a sermon has been written, it is ready. It is not. The writing is merely preliminary. As sermon, indeed, it does not at that stage exist at all. It is merely manuscript. The important thing is to re-absorb it, through your own person, into the context of God's saving purpose, so that it ceases to be a composition lying there on the desk, an " it ", and becomes part of you as a person, one soon to be a " thou ", God's " thou ", to another " I ". This reabsorption will be for most of us no easy matter. It will require an hour, an hour and a half, two hours, immediately prior to the service itself, working through it, pruning, correcting, rearranging, seeking to grasp it as a whole and to inform it with a clear awareness as to what is the major thing God would have you say, until it is in your mind and heart, and your mind and heart are in it. I would stress the importance of doing this—and what drudgery it can be—immediately prior to the service itself. For you, during that hour or two, the service has already begun. The very proximity of the preaching act makes you see your matter in a different light ; you hear yourself preaching it in a way that was not possible in the throes of composition. I have come to have great faith in changes made as it were with one foot already on the pulpit steps. I am not suggesting that the sermon should be learnt by heart, though I think I would rather that were done than that there should be no really costing effort to repossess it, to charge oneself with it, to give oneself " for Christ's sake and the gospel's " the liberty that comes only of mastery and the mastery that comes, for most of us, only of the drudgery of hard work. " For Christ's sake and the gospel's ", I repeat, for many have sought and found such free mastery and such masterly freedom in the sphere, and for the sake, of other far less important things. In this they put us to shame.

II

THE I-THOU RELATIONSHIP

I HAVE maintained that our conception of the preaching office and our theology are intimately bound up with one another. It is one test of preaching to ask how far it is in all its aspects consonant with your doctrine, and it is one test of your doctrine to ask how far it supports, informs, and makes sense of the act of preaching. My revered predecessor in Cambridge, Dr. John Oman, always expressed a strong disapproval of what he called "popular preaching". He was often misunderstood in this, partly no doubt because the word "popular" in this context needs definition. Some suggested that he was merely excusing his own obscure and difficult style in the pulpit. But this was certainly wrong. Oman's rejection of a certain type of preaching was part of his whole theological position. It was a manifestation of the powerful consistency and integrity of his personality. Had he had all the gifts that are necessary for a popular preacher in his sense of the term, he would still have shrunk from being one, for his whole understanding of God and man forbade it, and this understanding was part of himself.

I propose now to develop further the thought that preaching is only to be rightly understood and conducted when it is seen in the context of a Christian understanding of persons and their relationships with one another. It is first, last, and all the time a function of the personal world. I shall speak in this lecture of certain aspects of the world of persons in relationship, and in the subsequent lectures I shall make application to preaching of what thus comes before us. The time at our disposal being limited, and our interest being primarily in preaching and not in theology, there is no option but to lay down propositions in a somewhat dogmatic way, without staying to argue for them, or to take up any of the underlying problems. What is involved is nothing less than our whole doctrine of man and of the way in which God deals with man, especially in His saving work in Christ, and from this vast field I must be permitted to select only such truths as are related to the immediate purpose. Some of them I have argued for elsewhere. For the rest, if you think them open to question, or urgently in need of qualification, it may be that the application to preaching will still be of some value.

I begin with the proposition that God's purpose is such, and He has so made humanity in accordance with that purpose, that He never enters into *personal* relationship with a man apart from other human persons. When He confronts me in the specifically personal I–thou relationship, to use the phraseology referred to in the last lecture, it is always closely bound up with the personal I–thou relationship I have with my fellows.[1] I am related to the personal God in the neighbour, to the neighbour as personal in God.

It is perhaps not unimportant to insist that in saying this we are speaking of actualities and not merely of ideals. We are reporting the actual structure of the personal world as it has come forth from the creative hands of God. We are apt to think of this implication in one another of relations to God and relations to neighbour under the form of an ideal to be achieved, a commandment to be fulfilled. We think primarily of *right* relations which may or may not obtain, of the great commandment, Thou shalt love the Lord thy God and thy neighbour as thyself. But the ideal is rooted in the actual, the imperative rests upon the indicative, and what

[1] What is meant by a personal, I–thou relationship is discussed below, p. 41 f.

we are after here is not the ideal to be preached but the actual which all the time conditions the manner and power of our preaching.

We might express it by saying that when God created man He *eo facto* created an order or structure of persons in relationship with Himself and with one another. This is the ultimate secret of finite personal nature, of specifically human nature. Only as a man is part of, held in, that structure is he distinctively man. If, *per impossibile*, you could lift a man out of it, he would cease to exist as man. It is not that God creates a man and then pops him into the world of persons as a housewife makes a dumpling and pops it into the saucepan, both dumpling and saucepan being capable of existing apart from one another. To come into existence as a man is to be incorporated in this world of the personal, to be in relation to persons—the divine person and human persons—and existence as a man is not possible on any other terms.

It would be easy to interpret what has so far been said to mean that a man stands at one and the same time in *two* relationships which can in principle be separated from one another. On the one hand there is his relationship to the divine person, God, and on the other hand there is his relationship to finite persons, his fellows. Chris-

tian thought has not infrequently expressed itself
in terms which give countenance to such an idea.
The great commandment itself lends colour to
it—thou shalt love the Lord thy God *and* thy
neighbour as thyself. We speak of duties to
God *and* of duties to the neighbour. There is
Augustine's oft-quoted saying, "Thou hast made
us for thyself and our hearts are restless until
they find rest in thee." There is the whole
mystical tradition, of which Augustine's words
are probably in some measure an echo, that man
finds God by withdrawing from the world,
including the world of persons. Yet the true
Christian understanding is that these two relationships cannot ever be separated from one another.
Indeed it would perhaps be better to say that
there are not two relationships but only one
relationship which is twofold ; or, better still,
there is one personal continuum with two poles,
the infinite personal on the one hand, the finite
personal on the other. The individual is related
all the time to his neighbour in God and to God
in His neighbour, even when he is not aware
of it, even when he denies it, and in that relationship his distinctive quality as a human person
resides. So that Augustine's saying should be
rewritten, "Thou hast made us for thyself and
for one another and our hearts are restless until

they find rest in Thee in one another and in one another in Thee."

If this be so, then to say, as we have said, that God never enters into personal relationship with a man apart from other human persons is manifestly not in any way to set a limit to His power. Nor is there anything arbitrary about it. It is merely to report the created order as it is, and ultimately the reason why that order is what it is must lie in the inscrutable nature of the divine being itself. What is of God's will and nature cannot be limitation. Why God's creation of a finite person in relation to Himself requires other finite persons, so that the individual and his neighbour must come into existence together, why, in other words, it requires a historical process (for that is what history as distinct from nature is—the sphere of persons in relationship) it is in the last analysis impossible to say. It is part of the givenness of God, which in the end we must accept and ask no further questions.[1] But if it is accepted, we can discern in terms of it the necessity for the form which God's redemptive act towards the men whom He brings into

---

[1] It might be suggested that the necessity arises from the fact that God is Love. If in intending man God intended a finite being capable of sharing His nature and purpose as love, then *eo facto* a world of finite persons in relationship, *i.e.*, a historical process, is intended also, for love is meaningless apart from " persons in relationship ", and if love is an ultimate, then " persons in relationship " are also.

being by His primal creative purpose, in fact took, namely that of an historic incarnation in a human person and of the creation through Him of that order of redeemed personal relations which is the true Church. It is also possible, as we shall see, to discern the necessity for " preaching ". It is all part of the necessity of history, the necessity for God, being what He is, to approach a finite person through the medium of other finite persons.

If now I am asked to say more precisely what is meant by a personal relationship, by an I–thou relationship, to use Buber's terminology, I am in a difficulty just because we are here dealing with an ultimate in the world of being. An ultimate cannot be expressed in terms of anything else ; if it could it would not be an ultimate. But seeking to describe what must primarily be identified by each one in the immediacy of experience, it may be said that the heart of the matter is in the relationship of self-conscious, self-directing wills to one another in a situation which is important and significant for both. If you ask me what I mean by a " self-conscious, self-directing will ", I cannot say. I can only refer to your own immediate self-awareness. But it is possible to say something about the relationship between such wills which constitutes the specifically " I–thou " world. It is a relationship wherein the activity of one self-conscious, self-directing will is conditioned by that of another in such wise that each remains free. The last phrase " in such wise that each remains free " is almost tautological, for a will which was " non-freely " conditioned, *i.e.*, mechanically necessitated to do this rather than that, would not be self-directing, indeed it would not be a *personal* will, in our understanding of the term, at all, it would not be a " thou " to my " I ", but an " it ". We do, of course, in our sinfulness, try mechanically to control one another's behaviour and to force one another to do what we want, but the extent to which we can do this is limited. Always there is an inaccessible something in me which must give consent, in the light of what I myself see to be of value, to what you want. Even if you threaten me with unnameable tortures and death, I can still choose tortures and death and the last word is with me.

How then can your will condition mine so that my will remains free ? It can do so only by confronting me as an inescapable claim. Both words are important. I am free to reject it— that is why it is claim ; if I were not so free, it would be compulsion—but I am not free to escape it, for my rejection of it at once enters into the structure of history, your history, and in varying degree universal history. If the claim be a right claim, that is, one rooted in the essential nature of the personal world as this has been created by God, the rejection of it can have the most disastrous consequences. Herein, in part, lies the problem of atonement. The problem of atonement is the problem of setting right in a world of inaccessible, " non-manipulatable " wills the rejection of claims which is already part of history and at work in history. It is the restoration of the fabric of the I–thou world when it has been torn.

The idea of a claim, in the sense in which we are here using the term, is, I think, another indefinable. Its impact has to be felt to be known, and it is not analysable into other notions. It is the basis of the ethical concept of " ought ", which is also for that reason unanalysable, as Sidgwick insists. The ethical is the personal world, the world of history. One thing, however, we can say, and that is that a claim only conditions my will by being understood. I am free to accept or reject it, but I can only accept or reject it by first understanding it. I have not dealt with your claim at all if I have not understood it, if I have not grasped in some measure your world, your point of view, your meaning, and made it my own. This presupposes that though we see things from a different point of view—it is the differences of points of view that make claims possible—yet we are both in the same world and can speak and act in terms of it. This is but to say that reason and self-conscious, self-directing personality go together. By the same argument reasoning *together*, the possibility of, nay the necessity for, a community of insight and understanding, for shared meaning, is an essential part of the personal, the I--thou world.

In the light of these remarks it is possible to see how and why *speech* is so absolutely central and indispensable in the world of personal relationships. In view of what we have to say later about preaching, it is necessary to dwell on this for a little.

What a strange and potent thing speech is ! And how the familiarity of it hides from us its strangeness and potency ! We sometimes hear debated whether we would rather lose sight or hearing, if we were shut up to such a frightful option. The immediate reaction as a rule is to choose to retain the faculty of sight ; the thought of a permanently dark and colourless world affrights us. But I am not sure but what the wiser part would be to choose to retain hearing, for whereas the loss of sight would cut you off from all the loveliness and interest of the world of objects, the loss of hearing would cut you off from the world of persons, and there is no question which is the graver loss, which is the heavier blow at the innermost citadel of our being. The spoken word is right within the core of the I–thou relationship, and the written or printed word is always a poor substitute for it. Mankind seems to have instinctively known this from earliest times. Primitive peoples have a sense of the power of the spoken word which is exaggerated to the point of superstition, but which like many primitive ideas is founded on reality. We used to say in our childhood,

> Sticks and stones may break my bones
> But words will never hurt me !

Nothing could be more false. Words can and do hurt much more penetratingly and destructively than sticks and stones. Perhaps it was because deep down we knew that words can hurt most frightfully that we were so anxious to protest that they did not. The New Testament has a better understanding on the matter : " The tongue is a little member and boasteth great things. Behold how great a matter a little fire kindleth. And the tongue is a fire, a world of iniquity. So is the tongue among our members that it defileth the whole body, and setteth on fire the course of nature, and it is set on fire of hell ".   The absolute centrality of speech in the world of personal relationships is brought home to you when you are in a foreign country and know nothing of the language and nobody there knows anything of yours. Here you have in effect the frightful situation of both persons being deaf.[1] The sense of utter frustration and loneliness, of alienation and unreality, has to be experienced to be known.

The reason why the spoken word is thus at the very heart of the world of persons in relationship of the I–thou relationship, is that it is supremely that medium of communication wherein the three elements mentioned above, will and claim and shared meaning, are, or can be, at a maximum together in a single, fused unity.

Thus, first, in the spoken word my will objectifies itself for you with such force and immediacy that it and its objectification are one and indissoluble, almost indistinguishable. The word is my will, and my will is the word. This is clumsily and therefore inaccurately expressed, but a single

[1] When a foreigner fails to understand what we say, we instinctively raise the voice as though he were deaf.

consideration will show what I mean. Precisely at the moment when my will is withdrawn the word ceases as absolutely as annihilation. And it comes into being again just where and when my will ordains it. This is perhaps the nearest we get to the divine activity of creation out of nothing, and of preservation—pure creative and sustaining will.[1] It is this immediate dependence of the spoken word on the will that gives it its superiority over the printed word as a medium of personal relationship. What seems, what indeed from one point of view is, the advantage of the printed word, is that it can be listened to again and again whenever *I* choose— I have only to take the book down from my shelves and read it, and it can stay on my shelves a score or more years and not perish. This is precisely its disadvantage from the point of view of personal relationship ; for the essence of the personal relationship is in the activity of *your* will bringing the word into being and giving it the only being it possesses, not in the activity of my will.

The same would apply to a gramophone record of a man's speech. Here you hear the actual sound of the words, but the sense of an active

[1] How singularly apposite, therefore, the Johannine bringing together of the Word and Creation, and the identification made by later thinkers of the Logos and the creative principle.

will directly producing them and confronting your will through them is absent, or at least considerably diminished. What is giving the sounds their being is now only a whirling disc, and you can set it awhirling by your own will whenever you wish. Does not this explain the otherwise inexplicable fact—for I take it to be a fact—that a recorded broadcast of (say) the King's speech is not the same as to hear the broadcast itself? The voice, tone, inflexions are all there, but the sense of the creative will is fogged. The mechanism, with its capacity for infinite, undeviating repetition, gets in the way. Why, if one forgot to switch it off and left it, it might, subject only to the limitations of the mechanism itself, go on for ever ! Perhaps it is along similar lines that we can explain the fact that a typewritten, and still more a printed, letter seems in comparison with a written one, vaguely distant and impersonal. The writing of a word is only a little less immediately one with the creative will than the speaking of it ; the pen is hardly more than an extension of the fingers with their innervated muscles, and the style of writing is as individual almost as the voice itself. But the type machine, with its repeating mechanism, rises up between me and thee. The only activity which quite nearly approaches the spoken word as an immediate creation of the embodied will is the gesture and facial expression, but the limitations of these, particularly in relation to the points immediately following, are obvious. But this close affinity indicates why speech and gesture are so closely united and why the latter, if spontaneous and natural, is so great a help to effective oratory.

Second, and to be taken inseparably with what has just been said, in the spoken word you have in a maximal form the element of claim. When I speak to you my will claims yours. Speech is full of claim.

To begin with, I claim your attention. I should not speak if I did not want you to listen. By speech I ask you to listen. If you will not listen, I waste my breath, as the saying is. Sometimes when I have had occasion to rebuke one of my children, he stuffs his fingers into his ears. The result is a feeling of frustration and impotence in me which is not merely injured parental dignity and *amour propre*. It is as though the child had temporarily vanished, as though a thick wall, infinitely thicker than his puny little fingers, had come down between us. It is not that he has gone deaf, though that would be bad enough. He has *willed* to go deaf. He has repudiated my claim. That stopping of the ears symbolises, as nothing else can, the awful fact of freedom which lies at the heart of the personal world.   And dare we speculate that God gave us no lids for our ears as He did for our eyes, precisely that we might always be open to one another and to the word?

Then, further, by my speech I claim your answer.   My word, containing my will, is addressed to your will, and asks your answer containing yours, even if it be only the answer of a nod or a shake of the head.   I want response. It is a knock on the door—a call for attention which is also a call for an answer.

Then, again, there is implicit in my speech the claim of truth.   Thus there is within it, as there is in all personal dealings, the germ at least of the ethical.   Even when I speak to deceive you I rest upon the claim of truth to your allegiance ; my lies must have verisimilitude.   If neither of us acknowledges the claim of truth, personal intercourse is in so far forth as impossible as if we were both stone deaf.   Yet the fact that lies and deception are possible at all shows that we are in the region of claim and not of mechanical necessitation.

This, however, has already involved us in the third point, not to be separated from the other two, that the distinctive *raison d'être* of speech is to convey reasoned meaning, or meaning to reason and understanding. It is the supreme and distinctive vehicle of ideas, propositions, judgments, of truth in a form in which it can be, so to say, held at arm's length and considered. It may include other things in its intention as well, of course. Speech may be designed to excite feeling, or to create an æsthetic impression, or even, as in an advertising slogan, to affect, by repetition and sheer suggestive force, a man's actions almost without his knowing it, but in none of these things does its unique quality appear. Music can evoke feeling, a landscape or a flower can make an æsthetic impression, a forceful gesture or example can act as a powerful suggestion, without speech entering in at all. Speech is non-essential to these things. The unique function of speech is that of conveying in the most explicit way possible the judgment of one self-conscious awareness to another in such wise that both are brought directly and inescapably under the claim of truth. If it does, or seeks to do, any of these other things that we have mentioned—to stimulate feeling, to create æsthetic impression, to influence the will by force of suggestion—*without* doing this, it has not fulfilled its distinctive and noblest function, which, I repeat, is to convey truth in the form of an appeal from one personal insight to another under a common obligation to the truth.

I have elsewhere spoken of the way in which speech is adapted to this function of conveying meaning in such wise that the integrity of the personal judgment is respected, and perhaps I may be permitted here to quote some of my own words, as the point is not unimportant in relation to preaching.

" It is indeed ", I have said, " a highly significant fact that in the main men are able to communicate with one another only through signs and symbols. In more lowly forms of life it would appear to be otherwise. Rivers has suggested that ants and bees for example communicate and co-operate with one another through a process of suggestion so complete and irresistible that there arise the almost mechanically precise cohesion and collaboration of the anthill and the beehive. If this be so, it involves that such creatures have little of what might be called individual psychical existence at all. Their psychical being flows in and out of one another like a stream of water flowing in and around porous pots. There are no frontiers to their mental life, no, so to say, immigration barriers on the frontiers turning back undesirables. But nature seems also to have taken

another line. Along this line mutual permea-
bility of psychical being has grown less, the
frontiers have become more and more sharply
defined and policed, until in man in whom alone
appears anything that may truly be designated
individuality, or personal life, the isolation of
mind from mind is almost complete. Yet the
isolation only obtains in respect of that excess of
suggestibility which characterises other forms of
life. For man has elaborated a new method of
communication, one which allows full exchange
of meaning and yet respects the frontiers, the
territorial integrity of the personality, namely
the use of symbols, and particularly the use of
speech which is a highly complex and refined
way of signalling to one another. When I speak
to a friend, I cannot thrust my meanings directly
into his mind, however much I may be disposed
to think that it would be to his advantage if I
could. I can only come so far as the frontier
and signal my meaning, and the latter can only
become his after he has interpreted the signals
and taken up their significance into his own
personal awareness. He may, however, reject
their meaning, but the fact that it was first
symbolised is precisely what gives him the
opportunity to accept or reject it, to hold it so
to say at arm's length and consider it. Doubtless

we must not exaggerate this isolation of mind from mind even in respect of mere suggestibility. It does not require much observation to note how much people influence one another by suggestion without their being explicitly aware of it ; yet also it does not require much observation to note that it is precisely this open side of our being which is most inimical to the development of character and has most to be watched. It is well known that high suggestibility and low and unstable mental life go together." [1]

It is perhaps not superfluous to insist that I am not wishing to suggest that speech is the only medium for the conveying of truth from one personality to another. There are other symbols besides words and sentences, as, for example, those of music, art, ritual, and so on. Nor would I wish to restrict the category of truth only to those matters which can be expressed in propositional form. There is truth of feeling and valuation, and it is precisely this kind of truth that transcends verbal expression and requires other symbols. This is not the occasion to go into these matters, though I shall make incidental reference to them again later. But I do maintain that speech is superior to all other means of

[1] *The World and God*, pp. 70–72.

communication in that it unites, or can unite, in a maximal form that we have called will, claim and reasoned meaning, and so can be as nothing else can the medium of personal relationship.

III
PREACHING AS PERSONAL ENCOUNTER

WE have reached two main positions. The first is that God's personal approach to men and women is always through other persons, or, more generally, through history which is the sphere of persons in relationship, the sphere where decisions have to be taken and choices made in relation with other wills. Or, to put it differently again, God's I–thou relationship with me is never apart from, is always in a measure carried by, my I–thou relationship with my fellows. The second is that the I–thou relationship is a relationship between self-conscious, self-directing wills which condition one another through what we called " claim " and " shared meaning ".

I propose now to make application of these two positions to the subject of preaching. It will be convenient to take the second first, devoting to it this lecture ; the concluding two lectures will be given to some applications of the first.

If what has been said is sound, namely that speech is absolutely central and indispensable in the world of personal relationships, then we can begin to understand from a new angle why preaching is so central and indispensable in God's saving work among men. It is, as was indicated earlier, because He insists upon saving men as persons and in a personal way. And if the reason given why speech is so central and indispensable, namely that it is supremely that medium of communication wherein the direct confrontation of will with will through claim and shared meaning can be at a maximum, then we are in possession of a principle and a standard by which preaching may be judged. We may say that preaching is strong and effective precisely in the degree to which it combines these three things—will, claim, shared meaning—into a maximal unity. Not that other things are of no, or little, importance—subject-matter, felicity of language, clear arrangement and development of ideas, and such like. These are of very great consequence, though I shall not attempt to say anything about them, for they have been again and again dealt with more effectively than I can. Good matter, felicitous language, firm structure and arrangement, only become great preaching in proportion as they become, in the way that only speech can, the vehicle of a direct I–thou relationship between you and those you address, and so, in and through that, between God and those you address.

We will take up each of the three aspects, will, claim, reasoned meaning, in turn.

(1) First, the direct encounter of will with will.

I would lay it down as a general rule that anything which tends to minimise or muffle the impression that the preacher is speaking directly to the individual listener, as man to man, as the saying is, or, as we might say, as personal will to personal will, is to be avoided so far as the special conditions of preaching allow. It was said of somebody's preaching—was it White-field's?—that each person in his audience felt as though the message was intended for him and for him alone. That was high commendation, the highest possible commendation. We may put it another way by saying that the closer your sermon, in spite of the unavoidable limita-tions and difficulties, approximates to the natural and spontaneous directness of serious private conversation, the better preaching it will be. I say " in spite of all unavoidable limitations and difficulties ", because nothing can alter the fact that a public address is *not* a private conversation. I am suggesting only a regulative principle to be borne in mind. The more you can adapt the limitations of your medium to the personal approach, to the I–thou relationship, the greater your achievement. Queen Victoria, it is said, used to grumble that Gladstone always addressed her as though she were a public meeting. That was a legitimate complaint. No doubt a public meeting would have equally just cause for complaint if it were addressed merely as though it were a private person. The peculiar task of preaching, and that which makes it the extremely difficult thing it is to do well, is to combine these two things together.

What sort of thing is it which minimises or muffles the impression of direct personal relationship? I give some instances.

(a) First, and obviously, merely to read the sermon is fatal. It is worse than fatal ; it is a culpable repudiation of one's task and calling. This is so very obvious, and has been said so often, that there is no need to enlarge upon it, except to say this, that the alternative to reading is not dispensing entirely with notes or manuscript in the pulpit. The alternative to reading is *preaching* and you can *preach* from notes and even from the full manuscript, if you have taken the trouble to do what I spoke of earlier, namely to absorb it, and if your mind is dominated by the sense of this central I–thou relationship of which we have been speaking. I myself prefer on the whole to listen to a preacher who has some written matter with him in the pulpit. It gives the feeling that the man has really wrestled with, and thought out as in the presence of God, what God would have him say.

(*b*) Second, all rhetoric, all passages that even begin to have a purple tinge, all merely fine writing, all suggestion of literary preciosity should be suspect. Over them your blue pencil should hover instantly like a hawk over its prey. And you must put into that pencil something of the ruthlessness of the hawk, for it is precisely such passages, because you feel they might raise you above the ruck, that you will not want to let go or to prune. I would not wish to exclude anything that might be called eloquence. I would not wish to exclude, of course, feeling and the natural force and eloquence to which feeling, if it is sincere and springs from your being yourself gripped by the truth, may at any moment give rise. I would not wish to reduce the sermon to a prosaic matter-of-factness. Far from it ; but I am wanting to keep the direct personal relationship dominant, and I know it as a quite undeniable fact that the sort of thing to which I refer comes between the preacher as person and his hearer as person like a mist, and not less so because it is a very pretty mist with rainbow colours, and pleasant to contemplate.

In this connexion I would say, watch your adjectives. Ruthlessly cut out any adjective which is not absolutely essential to, and part of, the truth which you wish to convey. The superfluous adjective is to your message what barnacles and seaweed are to the clean straight lines of a ship designed to cut through the water like the edge of a knife. Why adjectives should thus tend to come between you and your hearer, muffling the encounter of will with will, I do not know, unless it be that in the natural speech of daily life when we have things of great moment to speak to one another about, we do not waste time and energy on frills. There is something incongruous too in staying to decorate the soul's encounter with the living God. Decoration and unreality wait closely upon one another, as the history of art clearly shows. Avoid, too, the unusual and purely literary word ; do not call a cup " a chalice ", or a box " a casket ", or green " verdant ". Compare, for example, this :

> Where streams of living water flow
> My ransomed soul he leadeth,
> And where the verdant pastures grow
> With food celestial feedeth.

with " He maketh me to lie down in green

pastures ; he leadeth me beside the still waters.
He restoreth my soul." Every noun in the
verse of the hymn has an adjective, and two of
them are literary—verdant, celestial. The effect
is somehow " muzzy " like light coming through
lattice work with creeper. The Scripture words
are strong, direct, simple, beautiful. The adjectives are necessary to the thought for in the East
greenness is rare and waters can be noisy and
turbulent.

(c) Third, be very sparing of quotations.
These, too, I am sure, tend to come between the
preacher and the hearer. I can only use the
word I have already used and say that they seem
in some way to muffle the personal encounter,
to make for the moment mediate and indirect
what should be as immediate and direct as
possible. Preaching is *you* speaking to a man's
heart and will—not Milton or Shakespeare or
anybody else, however great his name. I do
not propose that quotations should be completely
excluded, but they need to be used sparingly and
should always be short and relevant to the *main*
point you are making, not to some secondary or
incidental point. Nor, I think, if you must
quote, is it always necessary to give the source.
Perhaps it is only necessary when there is danger
of your being credited with what is not yours !

Even then it is not absolutely essential ; the anonymous formula " as has been said " or " as someone has said " is sufficient. The introduction of a proper name, especially if it is a well-known one, tends to divert the mind of the hearer not only from the content of what is being said, but also for the moment from the living person saying it. No doubt this is a small matter if quotation or reference are infrequent, short and to the point, but small matters make large if added together, and the warning is not unimportant for certain types of well-read, well-stored minds. A sermon too full of literary quotation or allusion is like a vessel with a thousand and one little leaks, each one negligible, but taken together they may drain it nearly empty. It is noteworthy that the sermons of F. W. Robertson, perhaps the greatest of modern preachers, are almost entirely bare of quotation and proper names.

(d) Fourth, do not be afraid to use the pronoun " you ", which is our common usage for " thou " and restores at once the directness of the I–thou relationship if in any degree this in the course of your argument has been lost. It would be wearisome to speak thus in the second person right through the sermon, indeed it is impossible if there is any development of a theme ; moreover, used too persistently and in the wrong way it might give an impression of " nagging " or " browbeating ", and of the preacher setting himself on a pedestal. Yet I am confident that such direct address should never be entirely omitted, as, according to my experience, it not infrequently is. If there is no point where you can say " you ", then it is strongly to be suspected that your discourse is not a sermon, but an essay or a lecture. It is at the points of focus, where you seek to draw your message together and drive it home in challenge or appeal or succour, that the pronoun " you " is indispensable ; but a wise preacher will take other opportunity that the development or exposition of the thought naturally offers for dropping into the second person. The utterly flat, impersonal, and insipid " one " should be avoided like the plague. And only a little less flat and insipid is the pronoun " we ", at any rate if too frequently used. Far better, if you want to associate yourself with your hearers to say " you and I " or " you and me ". It surprises me greatly how many preachers use the pronoun " we " almost continuously from start to finish. We feel this, the preacher says, we ought to do that, we naturally ask such and such a question. The result is that *we* get the impression that we are just sitting back and talking *about* God, whereas in effective preaching *you*, my friend, would be inescapably aware that God is talking to *you*, asking *you* questions which *you* must answer, offering *you* here and now the succour which *you* most desperately need.

I once heard this sentence in a sermon : "We learn from Jesus that the object of God's affection is man." I shall speak later of the danger of the abstract in preaching,[1] but I can illustrate that point in advance here along with the point we are now making concerning the use of " we " and " you ". " The object of God's affection "— how terribly abstract. " Man "—also abstract. " We learn "—whom does that refer to ? Now listen : " God says to *you* through Christ that He loves you, and you, and you, and all men." Direct, simple—concrete verb instead of abstract noun, God the subject and you another subject, the I–thou relationship.

(2) Second, the element of claim.

Concerning this I wish to say two things.

First, a sermon has failed, indeed it has not been a sermon, unless it carries to the serious hearer something of a claim upon, or summons to, his will, to his whole being as this gathers itself together in the will. A sermon, as we have already hinted, should have something of the quality of a knock on the door. A knock, we

[1] See Chapter IV.

said, is a call for attention in the first instance ; but it is also more than that, it is a call for an answer. We preachers might well have inscribed over our desks, the master text of all sermons as it were, the words : " Behold I stand at the door and *knock*." Yet how many sermons I have heard which lack this summoning note almost entirely. They begin, they trickle on, they stop, like the turning on and turning off a tap behind which there is no head of water. You who have listened have heard some statements about certain matters—very true statements, no doubt, and very important matters—but there has been no knock, indeed quite plainly no intention to knock. At best there has been only the rustle of someone's skirts passing the door. We might well set another motto over our desks alongside the one already suggested : " Please do not knock if an answer is not required ".

I am not suggesting that every sermon should be a continuous nagging at people, or should end with an impassioned evangelical appeal for that final decision for Christ which many of your hearers will have taken many years before. There are many types of sermons, and some will rightly be for the instruction, edification and confirming of the saints, rather than be directly intended for the conversion of sinners. Yet even in the instruction, edification and confirming of the saints the note of claim and summons should not be absent, though it will make itself felt in a different way. Almost everything depends on the mood and intention of the preacher and on his whole conception of his task. If his message has been prepared in the right way, with a clear and serious perception of the I–thou relationship which must lie at its heart if it is to be real preaching, the note of summons is certain to get through even though nothing is said about it in explicit terms. It must be realised that in this sphere of our life instruction without this note does not instruct, edification does not edify, confirmation does not confirm.

This leads me to the second thing I wish to say about the note of claim.

I do not believe that God ever comes livingly to a man or a woman without making a claim, a demand. Nor does He ever come without proffering strength and succour. The two, the demand and the succour, are inseparably one. I have written of this elsewhere and there is no need to develop it further here.[1] What I have in mind to say now is that I cannot avoid feeling that this austere element in God's approach to the soul, the element of claim and demand, is

[1] See *The World and God, passim.*

being dangerously minimised in much contemporary preaching.

There are two reasons for this. First there is the fact that these are terrible times in which we live, times of unspeakable worry and anguish for many people, times full of demand upon human resources almost to breaking point. It is natural, and indeed proper, that the preacher should feel that above all things else he wants to comfort, console and strengthen people with his message. But even so, the question is still to be asked, and we ought always to be asking it, not only in our preaching but also in our pastoral work, what is true comfort and consolation, God's comfort and consolation, for a human personality. The fact is, consolation which does not have at its heart a claim and a demand is not, for mature persons, consolation at all, nor can it be of God. Such consolation might be appropriate to a child, but not to a mature man. True consolation, consolation for mature persons, is not to have our immediate necessities and expectancies satisfied, but to have our deeper nature released. The only way to have our deeper nature released is to have a greater demand addressed to it, a demand in which our claim for comfort—or, let us say our " clamour ", which is the same word with the accent in the direction of noisy self-reference—is caught up and lost in God's claim upon us to seek first, last, and all the time, His kingdom. I believe that it is a profound and disastrous mistake, striking at the very heart of the gospel, to set the thought of God's judgment upon our sins, which is one aspect of His claim upon us, over against the thought of His comfort and consolation, and to suggest, as some appear to do, that when people come to church in these anguished times they are entitled to hear only, or mainly, about the latter. What comfort or consolation is there for us apart from the Cross, but do we really see the Cross if we see not in it God's condemnation of sin, not the sins of Germany only, but ours also? I am far from suggesting that God withholds his mercy from us until all claims are settled—that would be no gospel ; rather it is that by His very mercy He thrusts the claim again, and even more deeply, into our souls.

The second reason is the reaction of Christian thought in our time against the rather thin, pelagian, merely hortatory quality of some modern interpretations of the Christian message. The reaction is of course entirely right. Christianity is not just the setting up of lofty ideals and rigorous claims and exhorting people to follow them, and preaching which contrives to give the

impression that it is, is pitifully inadequate.
Christianity, and therefore preaching, is, as we
said in the first lecture, the announcement of
good news, of something that has happened, that
God has done for us men and our salvation ; it
is not the announcement of something that we
have to screw ourselves up to do. Yet to state
this truth, as I have often heard it stated, in the
form that Christianity is gospel not demand, is
very misleading. It is to set up an entirely false
antithesis. The question, as I have said, is
whether anything could be gospel for men which
is not in some central way demand also. No
doubt it would not be gospel if it were merely
demand, but equally much it would not be gospel
if there were no demand at all.

The fact is, something very near the heart of the
essential genius of Christianity is here at stake.
From one point of view this essential genius might
be stated in this form, that Christianity fuses God's
succour and God's demand indissolubly together.
It has been given through Christ the astonishing
insight which is the beginning of the solution of
all our problems, because it is the indispensable
basis of genuine reconciliation and the victory
that overcometh the world, that God's demand
is His succour and His succour is His demand.
" My meat is to do the will of Him that sent

me " The meat is not added as a reward for doing the will.

It would be possible to make a classification of all the religions of the world on this basis. There are those religions in which the thought of God as succour tends to dominate, to swamp, the thought of Him as claim. These are predominantly eudæmonistic ; God is primarily an adjunct and ally to man's desires for the good things of this life, corn and wine and oil. Then there are those in which the thought of God as claim and demand dominates and swamps the thought of Him as succour. These are predominantly ascetic, mystical, seeking the annihilation of our purposes and desires, even of the person itself. Then, again, there are those in which the thought of God as succour and the thought of Him as demand are in a sort of uneasy balance with one another ; you obey His demands here, and He will reward you elsewhere in proportion to your obedience. These are legalistic and ceremonial religions, religions of meticulous observance and nicely adjusted rewards and penalties. Finally there is our own faith where, as I have said, the two are fused together. The true blessedness of life is in doing God's will and in the fellowship with Him that such doing brings. This is a blessedness which no evil can defeat and no joy can corrupt.

I shrink therefore from any tendency to separate and set in antithesis to one another gospel and demand, and I bring the point in here to reinforce the statement that the element of claim must never be absent from your preaching. It must not in principle even be subordinate. It must be part of gospel, part of comfort. For, I repeat, in the end without God's claim gospel is not gospel and comfort does not comfort. I shall return to this from another angle in the last lecture.

(3) Third, the element of shared meaning. We saw that the distinctive quality of speech as a medium and vehicle of personal relationship is that it conveys meaning in such wise that the hearer is free to accept or reject it according to his own insight and sense of truth. Speech is an appeal to insight. It brings the hearer under the claim of truth. Only as such is it distinguishable from casting a spell or even from stimulating a reflex action like the knee-jerk. Do not the Americans speak of a certain type of hypnotic orator as a spellbinder?

Clearly the preacher, if he is to sustain his solemn responsibility for creating that I–thou relationship with his hearers in which the divine

Thou Himself approaches men and women, cannot permit himself to lose sight of this. He must indeed be always out for a verdict in the heart of his hearers of so profound a kind that both feeling and will are involved, and not for merely a hearing of the polite Athenian type which says " we will hear thee again of this matter " ; but it must be a genuine verdict and not a merely reverberatory echo of other people's feelings and convictions. The preacher must deeply reverence in his hearer what has been called the sacred power of rejection, even in the midst of his passionate desire for acceptance. This means, among other things, that the preacher must himself have a profound reverence for the truth and must take care that in his desire to drive home his main message he never succumbs to the temptation of making statements which are unverified and unverifiable and will not bear critical examination. Such carelessness, even on small matters, quickly destroys confidence. That is one reason why honest and sound exegesis of the text is so important. To twist a text to your message, even if it be a great and true message, imparts a flavour of sham and pretence to the whole thing. Samuel Butler spoke once of the " irritating habit of theologians and preachers of telling little lies in the interest of a great truth ". This is worth remembering.

All of this, in general, I take to be obvious. But in practice there are difficulties and problems, two of which we may not unprofitably consider.

(*a*) The first is the problem of the right relation of what may broadly be called feeling, or perhaps we should say feelings, emotions, to the perception of religious truth and the evoking of religious decision.

What we have in mind may perhaps be best indicated by its more extreme examples, though these are so extreme that they constitute for most of us no problem. The hot-gospelling meeting most of us feel to be quite certainly wrong, the wrongness not being any the less because the preacher who conducts it is in real earnest, sincerely believes what he says, and has a genuine and not merely an egotistic desire for the conversion of men and women. The deliberate and unrestrained whipping up of feelings, the exploitation of mass influence, the use of words and phrases and hymns primarily because of their emotional associates and only secondarily, if at all, because of their meaning—which indeed is hardly examined at all, the massing of what might be called suggestive artillery at the appropriate moment when the hearer has been brought into his most susceptible state, all the barriers being down and his powers of resistance at their weakest—all this we know is an abuse of the human person. It is to degrade what should be the highest relationship between God, man and his fellows to the most crude and mechanical impersonalism. It is the propaganda of the Nuremburg Nazi meeting translated into gospel terms. A young friend of mine, in his adolescent years thought he was converted at such a meeting. He stood up and testified and signed a card. It was some years before he finally came out of the wilderness into which that experience led him, before he shook off the intense sense of personal degradation which, he told me, took possession of him the very next day.

That right feeling is an indispensable element in the perception of, and response to, truth in the sphere of persons, and above all in the sphere of that saving truth which is in Jesus Christ, is not open to question ; but the problem is, how may we evoke feeling so that it *is* right and plays a proper and not improper part ; how may we use it so that it supports and informs real insight, and does not merely create a false and degrading substitute for it. Consider, for example, the place and function of music. I confess I am a little afraid of music. It can so easily stimulate emotions far beyond any point to which real insight and genuine decision of will would ever take them. I have heard music which flooded my soul with heroic feelings, but these have vanished like mist so soon as the music has stopped. I have heard a military band with rolling drums which has filled even my pacific soul with martial ardour and evoked a strong desire to have a whack at someone or something, I knew not what. I suspect that in church many a man has mistaken the oscillation of his diaphragm in harmony with a ten-foot organ pipe, or the quivering of his heart strings to the melting sweetness of a boy's voice, for a visitation of the Holy Spirit. And there are other ways of working on the emotions—ritual, vestments, the vast grandeur of Gothic cathedrals, the dim, romantic light of stained glass, the cunning artifices of modern flood lighting. And the preacher, if he have certain gifts, a hypnotic eye, a magnetic presence, a numinous voice, a solemn unction, aided perhaps, as I have once or twice observed it, by a darkened building and one spot-light over the pulpit, can take his place in the scheme.

Yet none of us would wish to deny that there is a legitimate place for music, as for beauty of architecture and ritual, and if one has a numinous voice rather than a shrill and metallic one, it is surely none the less a gift for being, as most gifts are, not without its danger. There are problems here intimately concerning our work which I think do not have sufficient thought given to them ; but even if I were capable of discussing them profitably, this would not be the occasion to do it. I limit myself to two remarks, which have to do with our special interest in preaching.

First, that so far as the service generally, of which preaching is a part, is concerned, the main safeguard is for it to be governed by the spirit of worship. That is to say it should be directed all the time outwards towards God and not inwards towards our own feelings about God. It should be objective and not subjective in direction. Any piece of music or ritual which is deliberately and primarily designed to stir people's feelings and not to express, and by expressing to deepen, the apprehension of God is dangerous and should be suspect. The motive which governs the writing and choice and rendering of music or hymn or liturgy is here the important thing, and inevitably makes itself felt in the result. If the eyes are fixed on God, as in the clean, objective music of Bach, that is one thing ; if they are fixed on people's feelings about God, as in the mushy sentimentalism of some of our hymns, that is another and entirely different thing. The good leader of praise is the man who is so within the act of worship that he *has* to choose the right music to carry and sustain and express it ; the bad leader of praise, though he have every technical skill, is the one who, with equal seriousness of purpose, says to himself: " What can I play to create an atmosphere ? " and would dearly like to catch a glimpse of people's faces, if he could, to see whether he has been clever enough to do it.

Yet even when we have said this, great difficulties remain. For in the first place it is all too easy to have wrong and inadequate ideas of God, and in the second place we all in varying degree bring such disordered and uninstructed minds to worship that we are quick to twist everything in a subjective direction and to judge even the most clean and objective ritual, not by the degree in which it confronts us with the reality of the divine nature and will, but by the degree in which it gives us feelings of an expansive and pleasant kind. No doubt it is sometimes only poverty of language which makes our first comment that we *enjoyed* a service, and not " I saw the Lord high and lifted up ; woe is me ! I am a man of unclean lips ". No doubt we have all felt qualms in using the word or in hearing it used, but many I fear do not feel any qualms at all. The supreme test for them really is whether they have found the hour in church enjoyable, whether the music being good, the singing hearty, the decorations no offence to the eye, the curtains the right shade, the building beautiful, they come away " feeling " better. The sense that truth, saving truth, the truth that liberates, is at once infinitely valuable and infinitely difficult to come by for our sin-darkened minds is almost completely absent. I have sometimes caught myself wondering whether aspirin would not have served just as well.

Now it is here that preaching plays its all-important and indispensable part, which is the second thing I want to say in this connexion. The prime function of speech between me and thee is to convey truth in such wise that it becomes really thine. It can, as I have said, do other things, stir feelings, evoke æsthetic satisfaction by its beauty and order of conception and form, impart worthy suggestions which may later bear fruit almost without the hearer knowing it—I am not wishing to exclude anything—but its prime function is to help a man to *see*. It is the sermon, therefore, which can do more than anything else, under God, to keep the whole transaction of worship, so full of pitfalls and dangers, on the highest level of personal relationship, making it clean and objective with truth and bringing the whole thing to a focus in the response of the will to the will of God. Hymns, doubtless, can play a part ; but hymns are apt to be too familiar, to run too smoothly in the well-worn grooves of the mind, and they have emotional overtones and associations which may deceive us. The readings from Scripture suffer from the drawback of being either unintelligible, so that we read into them our meanings, or so familiar that they run through the mind like water over pebbles. No doubt it is possible also to read our own meanings into the sermon, or to fog and distort its message by the clamour of our own feelings, but if the preaching is both forceful and true, this is not so easy, to say the least. The speech of another person is a direct check and challenge, a thrusting into the current of my own habitual thoughts from outside, in a way that nothing else in the service can be.

From this angle the wisdom of the reformers appears in always associating the speaking of the word with the other sacraments, and the protestant habit, which is sometimes derided, of always having an address at every meeting is seen to have sound reason behind it. It is part of our whole understanding and valuation of the person and the personal way in which God deals with him, part also of our keen realisation of the deceitfulness of the human heart, which can hide from God even in the very act of praise and prayer, and set up in His place an idol of its own creation. I want the thrusting intrusiveness, the interjection, of another's serious speech. I always feel this to be a great lack when I come from a Quaker meeting that has been gone through in complete silence. I am sure I have worshipped, but I come away with the sense of having been far too much shut up in my own poor thoughts to be good for me.

I, for one, then, believe that there can be no substitute for the sermon, and I have little sympathy with the tendency in some quarters today to minimise it, and even to suggest we might get rid of it altogether. I do not agree that we have made too much of it in the past. Our mistake has been not to make enough of the other part of the service and to train our people in worship and in an understanding of the function of the Church, so that they can see the true nature of the sermon and its relation to the whole, above all its relation to their own calling and destiny as personal beings. I am not averse from methods other than the sermon being used to present the message of Christ.   Let there be religious films, if they can be worthily made ; let the drama be used, if it can be effectively presented ; I am all for wise experiment.   But let not these, or anything else, ever be allowed to exclude the direct spoken word of the I to the thou.

I observe that in his last film *The Great Dictator* that strangely wise little man Chaplin comes forward at the end and makes a speech to the audience.   I observe too that the critics nearly all say that this is a mistake, that Chaplin preaching is out of harmony with the character he bears in the rest of the film, that the artistic quality of the whole is thus broken.   They may be right, but I am sure Chaplin is even more right.   Chaplin felt he had something to say to his contemporaries and he was not going to trust even his own film to say it.   It is as though he says to the audience : "You are not going away having merely laughed and enjoyed yourselves, or with one or two vague feelings of dislike for the dictators, and hopes for the future.   I have got something to say of the utmost importance. I want to get it on to your wills.   I must speak to you direct.   Let artistic unity go hang.   I must preach."

You must then prepare your sermon and

preach it with your mind filled with the thought that it is your supreme task to convey truth so that these people see it genuinely for themselves and respond to it because so seeing it they, as self-directing persons, can do no other. You must not aim primarily at stirring feelings or leaving a deep impression ; that way danger lies not only for your hearers, but for your own soul. You may well hope that there will be right feeling, that there will be a deep and lasting impression, but you must leave that to God. It is not committed to your care.

(*b*) The second problem is the problem of the authority of the preacher.

The position we have been maintaining might well raise in our minds the question whether it will not, in proportion as it is taken seriously, take away from our preaching the note of confidence and authority. On the one hand the appeal to the insight of the hearer, the desire not to take him any farther than his own sincerest judgment will take him, might have the result that we speak with a certain hesitating diffidence, with in fact altogether too much deference to the judgment of sinful men and women, part of whose sinful situation is that they flee from the truth and will not face it, indeed may have lost all capacity to judge it. You do not, it may be said, appeal to the insight of a drowning man ; you drag him out, and if he struggles you may have to give him for his own good a mighty blow under the chin. On the other hand, it might be suggested, this deference to the other man may undermine our confidence in our own message. Am not I a fallible sinner also ? What right have I to speak with confidence about the deep things of God to my brother man ? The result will be that we preach not with the resounding, sum-moning, prophetic " Thus saith the Lord ", but with a " on the whole I think, and I hope you will agree with me, that under the circumstances it is probably true to say——"

If this were indeed the inevitable consequence of what we have been saying, it would be serious. Certainly the note of authority must never be lacking in our preaching if it is to be strong and effective and true to its message, for two reasons at least.

First, only thus can it meet the reality of man's need. The cry for firm and trustworthy direction as to what a man should do and believe may sometimes have a perverted origin and find a perverted satisfaction. It may spring from an infantile attitude to life, a fear to launch out and take the risks and responsibilities of maturity, a yearning for the lost comfort and protection of mother's bosom. It may issue in complete and even joyful submission to external dictation, as in the Roman Church or, infinitely worse, in the totalitarian state. Yet the cry is too persistent and poignant to be wholly perverted. It does spring from the reality of the human situation. Even the seers and saints, who know so much more than we of the immediate certainties of intercourse with God, bear witness to this. Sin is always with us and sin obscures God. Terrible things happen, as in these grim days, and the soul begins to doubt the truth of its highest vision. Testing situations arise when a man is called to stake even his life, and then he begins to waver and to ask for some other assurance than his own conviction that the sacrifice he is called upon to make, involving possibly others whom he loves, is really sane and worth while. It is these facts of man's spiritual immaturity and spasmodic and erratic growth into the truth, his muddled insights, his shadowed and chaotic life, his sinful failures and disloyalties—everything in his nature and experience that clouds and obscures vision— which bring it about that throughout the history of Christianity there has been a cry for an external authority which shall make up for the woeful deficiencies of a man's own inner light. We believe ; help our unbelief. We thought we knew and were sure, but now we are paralysed with doubt ; give us certainty. Our inner light is but a guttering, windblown candle in the vast, dark, boggy places of the moor ; give us from some blazing sun outside ourselves the comforting certainty and lucidity of the day. Tell us once and for all what we must believe, what we must do, what we may hope for.

And then, second, a note of authority in our preaching is essential if it is to be true to its message. For Christianity is a religion of revelation ; its central message is a declaration, a proclamation, that God has met the darkness of the human spirit with a great unveiling of succouring light and truth. The revelation moreover is historical, that is to say, it is given primarily through events which in the first instance can only be reported and affirmed. As we have already said, no merely internal reflexion can arrive at historical events. If a man is to be saved he must be confronted again and again with the givenness of Christ.

The note of authority then must not be absent, least of all in these days when everything is in dissolution and into the vacuum of men's despair and uncertainty there are rushing a number of new dogmatisms of the most violent and ill-founded kind. And nothing we have said need involve its absence. But we must ask what sort of authority is it that should inform our speech, what sort of authority truly succours the soul of mature man? Is it to be one which seeks to override, claims submission, is impatient with the questions and hesitations of active and resilient, or fumbling and muddled, minds, or one which seeks to quicken and succour insight, one which really believes in the Holy Spirit and in the light that all the time is seeking to lighten every man that cometh into the world? Must we not repudiate entirely the suggestion that there is any incompatibility between confidence in our own message and the most firm insistence that a man must walk by his own insight all the time? The measure of our willingness so to insist is indeed the measure of our confidence in the truth of what we say. The dogmatist is not infrequently a fugitive from his own doubt and unbelief.

The vital difference, as Oman used to say, is between speaking with authority and speaking from authorities, and the great exemplar is the Master Himself, of whom it was said that He spoke with authority and not as the scribes. If any one ever had the right to impose Himself and His message by overriding authority upon men, He surely had it. Aware of the final decisiveness of His own person in the destinies of men, announcing the breaking in of the eternal kingdom of God upon history in His own advent, taking to Himself the highest category in the religious thought of men, there is nevertheless a complete absence of any attempt to compel men's allegiance whether by threat or command or any form of prestigious suggestion. Indeed there is a manifest shrinking from any such thing. " Yea and why even of yourselves judge ye not what is right ? " He cried. " Be ye not called Rabbi, for one is your teacher ". " He that hath ears to hear, let him hear." In this last oft-repeated formula how much, how very much, is contained of the unique and distinctive quality of Christ, of His whole understanding of God and of the way of His coming to man.

All of this perhaps is superfluous in the ears of those who have been brought up in the Reformed tradition ; yet I do not know. There are not lacking signs of a tendency to match the over-riding authoritarian dogmatisms of contemporary ideologies with a like dogmatism in the assertion of the Christian message, a like depreciation and suspicion of the individual judgment, a like " take-it-or-leave-it " attitude, anyone who elects to leave it being set down either as wilfully recalcitrant, or more likely as still hopelessly lost in the fogs of an individualistic, self-confident, and outmoded liberal modernism. I observe in some, especially in some of my younger friends, what seems to me an extremely dangerous confusion of the *content* of what a man believes with the *manner* of his coming to believe it. An individualistic philosophy of life of the kind that dominated so much of nineteenth-century thought and practice we all agree is false and disastrous ; but an individualistic view of the act of believing, in the sense that in the end the individual must walk by his own insight, poor as it may be, or else be shorn of his proper manhood, seems to me to be axiomatic. Even if you say to a man, you have no right to set up your private judgment against the whole weight of the authority, say, of the Christian Church, you can only say it, and wait and hope that he will agree with you, so that his private judgment, the inner sense of what is fitting and true, remains the final arbiter. The trouble is not that men walk by their own insight, but that they walk without humility, and in narrow places where there are no broad horizons of history, and under the distorting influence of subconscious fixations and inhibitions. But the cure for that is to teach them to walk with humility, to set their feet in a larger room, to release them from themselves—not to ask them

G

to cease walking by their own insight altogether. And all this God can and does do through the gospel of His love, as it comes through Christ and borne on the witness of His people, the Church.

How may we have within ourselves that which shall impart to our preaching the right sort of authority, the conviction and confidence which lacks neither a proper respect for the hearer nor the humility of a sinful man, which is neither overridingly dogmatic nor weakly diffident and hesitant? I suppose in the end the secret lies in the quality of our own spiritual life and the extent to which we are ourselves walking humbly with God in Christ. But apart from that, it is perhaps of some help to remember two things.

The first is that after all any one sermon is only a small part of our total ministry, even of our total preaching ministry. It is not necessary to speak every sentence, every paragraph, or even every sermon, with the same ringing note of conviction, for your witness as a whole to have under God great weight and power. Of course there must be some basic convictions into which, when you speak of them, there will be poured your whole soul, for otherwise you should not be in the ministry at all; but, for the rest, there may be distinct gain in sometimes confessing your ignorance and hesitations and doubts and fears. Your hearers will gain, not lose, confidence in you from your frankness and from the sense that you are a learner and traveller with them. Moreover it is good that both preacher and hearer together should acknowledge the mysteries of life and of God. *Deus cognitus, deus nullus.* A theology that knows every mortal thing is a sham.

The second thing is that just as any one sermon is only a part of your total ministry, so also your total ministry is only a part of the whole witness of the Christian Church. There is a sense in which you cannot and must not speak beyond your experience and conviction ; if you do, an accent of unreality will assuredly creep in and you will unconsciously become dogmatic in the bad sense, seeking to hide your insincerity from yourself as well as from your hearer by the vigour of your utterance. But there is another sense in which you will never be able to speak except beyond your own experience and conviction. For you speak always out of the bosom of the Christian Church, and behind and within your every utterance there is the witness of a historic process running back to those whose eyes first saw and whose hands handled the Word of life—infinitely larger than you, longer than your short years, and much more universal than the contingencies of your personal biography.

I am sure that is so, and I am sure that people are aware almost subconsciously that that is so. It is, though the analogy is perhaps in some ways not too happy, a little like our reaction to the policeman. He may be a very unimpressive person in himself, with no experience beyond the confines of the village, and in general ill-informed and stupid, but there confronts us in him, and we know it though we might not put it into such terms—no, not the majesty of the law—but the long history, the stored experience, the social solidarity of the English people. In like manner, though in a different mode, it is the context of the preacher which entitles him to speak with confidence and be heard with respect, even though he be the rawest theological student. That is one reason why the sermon has a context in the service itself; we are invited to sing the hymns, to join the prayers, to hear the scriptures of the universal and age-long Church. The preacher's Christian experience is not self-contained or self-maintained. It comes into being, and is maintained in being, by its participation in an organic continuity of Christian experience and history, and however thin and poor it be, it carries something of the weight and power of that larger reality, just as even a blunt spear point still has behind it the weight and power of the shaft.

IV

THE NEED FOR CONCRETENESS

WE turn now to make some application to preaching of the first of the two main positions which we have already laid down,[1] the position namely, that God's saving approach is always through persons in relationship, or, more generally, through history which is the sphere of persons in relationship.

And, first of all, this truth reminds us that the act of preaching is part of a larger system of personal relationships and cannot be rightly understood in separation from it. The preacher, his sermon and his hearers are embedded in this larger system, and what the preaching effects largely depends upon it.

In other words, preaching is essentially a pastoral activity. It is part of a pastoral relationship, one activity of a settled and continuous ministry. I am in entire agreement with Mr. Charles Smyth on this point. In his interesting book *Preaching in the Church of England from* 741 *to* 1939, he quotes a mediæval handbook of instruction, the *Regimen Animarum :* " Who can

[1] P. 37.

lawfully preach ? ", it asks, and the answer given is, " Priests, deacons and sub-deacons who have the care of souls ".[1] That is a piece of ancient wisdom which is still valid and important. Those who have what are called " pulpit gifts " will suffer great loss of power if their preaching is not surrounded by those more direct and intimate personal relations which are part of a faithful pastoral ministry exercised over a number of years. And to succumb to the temptation to rely on your pulpit powers to make up for deficiency on the pastoral side is fatal. In the end it leads to what I can only call " French-lacquer " preaching, bright and interesting, but lacking depth and tenderness and searching power. It takes on the brassiness which the Apostle said characterises even the speech of angels when there is no love. You cannot love men from the pulpit. You can only love them in concrete personal situations wherein there is cost.

On the other hand for those of us who have no marked pulpit gifts there is surely here great encouragement. Our preaching, poor as it may be, can gain power and effectiveness if it comes to people out of the heart of a true and deep pastoral, that is personal, relationship, though this, needless to say, must not be taken as an

[1] P. 4.

excuse for not taking trouble by hard work to make the best possible use of such powers as we have. It is not merely that to be close to your people in their daily situations and thoughts gives you matter to preach upon ; that is perhaps the least important thing, though it is not unimportant. It is that only thus can you yourself grow in knowledge of the deep things of God, for I repeat the primary medium of God's revelation is history, is the personal order in which we are with one another, and not the commentary, or the theological work, or the comfortably insulated study.

I have not myself great confidence in the isolated sermon of the type which I am by the circumstances of my life compelled to preach, the sermon preached by what the Americans call a " guest preacher ", here today and gone tomorrow, like a mendicant friar. It would be foolish to suggest that God can never use such incidental preaching, but I feel confident, for the reasons given, that it is one of the lesser media of His grace, and one of those we could with least loss dispense with. It may be asked, What of the evangelical address, say, in the open air to people who have no connexion with the church and its pastoral ministry ? But this illustrates my point rather than questions it. For anybody who has engaged in this sort of preaching knows how urgently it requires what is called " follow-up work ", *i.e.*, it requires to be incorporated at once into a context of direct personal relationships.

All this makes evident how much the effectiveness of our preaching does depend on the sort of persons we are, as manifested in our personal dealings. No doubt we must insist that the efficacy of the sacraments as " means of grace " does not depend on the personal quality of the celebrant, but I doubt whether we ought to state that truth in too unqualified a form, whether we ought not to state it only in the modified form that the personal quality of the celebrant can never, in God's mercy, reduce the sacrament to a nullity for any who come in sincere and humble faith. For it seems to me to be the plain declaration of experience, and no theology ought to go against the plain declarations of experience, that when the personal relations of men and women who gather round the Lord's Table are wrong, there is a manifest and inevitable loss of sacramental power, even for those who are not directly responsible. At any rate I am sure that the Holy Spirit has a much harder task to bestow its gifts upon me, if, say, the minister and his elders are in any sort of wrong personal relationship to one another. To suppose otherwise, to abstract the whole transaction too completely from the personal quality of the participants, is to run grave danger of depersonalising the whole thing and of thinking of the individual in quite false abstraction from the neighbour with whom he constitutes the personal order and apart from whom he would not be human at all.

But, however that may be in relation to the sacraments of Baptism and Holy Communion, I am quite sure that what I have been saying holds of what in a looser sense of the term sacrament has been called the sacrament of the word—preaching. The saying " I cannot hear what you say, because what you are shouts too loudly " is here justified. No doubt it ought always to be remembered that the preacher is a sinner, needing forgiveness, like everybody else, that the sermon is as much a message to him as to those who listen, but it is flying in the face of facts to pretend that the discrepancy between the preacher's message and what he is known personally to be is of no consequence. It is of consequence, and it ought to be of consequence. This is a burdensome and challenging thought, but we must not run away from it.

Yet the burden and the challenge of it, perhaps it is worth while to pause and say, are not for the preacher alone.   They are for the congregation also, and it is a pity that this is not more often realised.   The congregation has a responsibility for the effectiveness of the sermon, for they also are part of the system of personal relationships in which the sermon is, as it were, a focalisation and by which it is carried.   They are, or are meant to be, the Fellowship of the Spirit, which is the organ of God's saving activity in the world. The fellowship is a means of grace not to be isolated from other means of grace.   Every minister knows how some congregations seem to give power to the preacher, whereas others seem to inhibit it in greater or less degree.   An intrinsically poor address can become a strong word of God when it is part of, and expresses, a strong and deep fellowship of God's people, who come wakeful, expectant, teachable, prayerful, humble, into God's presence.   On the other hand an intrinsically good sermon may be ineffective, or at least nothing like so effective as it might be, if the congregation is not a fellowship, but only a crowd of unresponsive, apathetic folk, wanting above all things else not that God's word should have free course among them even through the lips of this man, but that they should be interested for twenty minutes or so.   Ready, if they have been bored, to grumble over the dinner table as though they had been cheated out of something they had bought and paid for. And it is not only lovelessness on the part of the preacher that turns him into a sounding brass and a tinkling cymbal. It is lovelessness in the church, for preaching is an act of the church. " I cannot hear what you say, because what the congregation is shouts so loud."

Yet, even so, it would be a mean thing for us preachers to blame our congregations for our ineffectiveness.

Then, next, the fact that the medium of God's approach to the human spirit is the world of personal relations warns us of the necessity for concreteness in our preaching. This is a matter of such importance that I propose to dwell on it at some length.

I believe that abstractness in some ways is the greatest curse of all our preaching ; I speak as a great sinner in this respect. But the reason why it is a curse, the reason why the dealer in abstractions is bound to be a failure, is not always understood. The reason usually given is that if we are too abstract people will not understand us, or will be uninterested and bored. There is no doubt a great deal in that, but there is a deeper reason, a reason which would hold even if you did succeed in making your abstract statements both intelligible and interesting, the reason just given, namely that God comes at people not through abstractions at all, but through persons and through the concrete situations of day to day personal life. There is indeed a type of mind, especially of educated mind, which finds great delight in the development and interplay of abstract theological ideas and general theological truths, if it is at all skilfully done, and for such minds it can be a positive snare and danger. The play of ideas screens them from the living God. It is an escape from God the more dangerous because it professes to be an encounter with Him. It would have been better perhaps to be like the simpler folk in the congregation and be merely bewildered and bored by the sermon.

The need for concreteness applies, of course, in the first instance to phraseology. I am sure that we ministers do not realise how abstract our terminology is, what semi-technical jargon we are always using, such as the ordinary man, who has never been through a theological college and never reads a theological or even a religious book, cannot be expected to understand. But, I repeat, it is not merely a question of not being understood. Even if we are understood, there is apt to be something wrong with the abstract word.

It lacks a certain tang and flavour of the real historical world where we see and hear things and where we have above all to *do* things. That is why American speech, and Americans are all active people, is so strangely refreshing, and even at times disconcerting. We in Britain like things draped, and we call it refinement and politeness. We put up over a stall or shop " refreshments " ; the American puts up " eats ", and when you read the word, instantly you can see men inside munching their steak. We put up " no admittance " ; the American puts up "keep out ", and instantly your whole sensory-motor system jumps and quivers in response. We put up at a railway crossing " the public is warned that it is dangerous to cross the line "; the American puts up " stop, look, listen ! " (These two last instances, by the way, illustrate what I have already said about the superior force of the direct I = thou form of address.)[1] We speak of " the necessity for a mutual adjustment of plans ", the American says " I must gear my plans in with yours," and instantly you see oiled and interlocking cogwheels and shafts. Curiously the American, I have observed, is apt to lose this in his preaching and to betake himself to polysyllabic and latinised abstractions ; yet it is not

[1] P. 63.

so curious, but rather illustrates the more the
danger of which I speak.   For if he can succumb
to this blight, how much more we, who have the
habit in our daily conversation ?

I counsel you therefore to go through your
sermon when it is written and look hard and long
at every abstract word.   Often it will not be
possible to alter it to a concrete word, for abstract
terms are part of the indispensable coinage of
thought and even the simplest mind uses them ;
but it may be possible to alter it to one more
familiar.   Yet even so, it is surprising how often
an abstract term can be altered to a concrete,
and how great is the resultant gain in vividness
and power.

Recently in a sermon I wrote these words :
" Is not faith in God mature in proportion as it
is governed by the thought of Him as absolute
holiness.   On the other hand is it not immature
in proportion as we are able to unite the thought
of God with a purely comparative morality ? "
Fortunately the Spirit pointed out to me what a
monstrosity that was.   I was able to rewrite
it thus : " Is not faith in God mature according
as a man never forgets that God is utterly holy
and of too pure eyes to behold iniquity ?   Is it
not immature according as a man is able to come
into the presence of God comparing himself

with others or with what he himself once was ? "
The new form is perhaps not very good, but it is
definitely an improvement.

But the need for concreteness applies not only
to phraseology ; it applies also, and even more,
to the content and presentation of the message.
We must have the deliberate intention, and make
a deliberate effort all the time, to " gear " the
truth into the actual life-situations of men and
women today, so that those who listen will be
unable not to see their own world coming
through the message as a pattern is brought out
in an otherwise featureless fabric by a hot iron.
A sermon on Jacob at Bethel has failed if someone
has not been brought to see the ladder " pitched
betwixt Heaven and Charing Cross ", or on
Christ coming to His disciples in need, if He has
not been seen " walking on the water, not of
Gennesareth but Thames ".

I say *the deliberate intention and the deliberate effort*,
for such " gearing in " will not happen of itself.
It is no easy task. I marvel sometimes not that
preaching is so bad, but that it is not worse.
For there are still other difficulties besides the
difficulty of our incurable abstractness, our
inordinate love of generalisations which gains all
men's consent and stings nobody's conscience.

Thus there is the difficulty that we preach from

the Bible. Our task is to confront men and women with the Living God, the God who speaks through, and asks their obedience in, this present world of automobiles, aeroplanes, radio, cinemas, big business, machine industry, mass democracy and totalitarian war. But the first thing we do is to take them to a remote past and a distant and strange world of men and women who speak another language, think in other categories, face other problems. I know it can be argued that in some ways this is an advantage, that in the simpler world of the Bible we can see the ultimate issues of our life more clearly than in the tangled complexities of the present age. I know that the Bible is unique among books, that the spirit of God can and does most mysteriously speak to our present condition and situation through it. I am aware that according to our faith and experience the Christ who walked in Palestine is our contemporary now—identically the same Christ—and that in Him is the final secret of all history, so that it is not quite true to say we have to leap over the centuries into another world ; rather we are laid hold of by One who is somehow the centre of all history, the same yesterday, today and for ever. I know the ultimate certainties here, in which all that is distinctive of the Christian revela-

tion consists. I know something of the theological doctrines which seek to comprehend those
certainties, in spite of the underlying problems,
in a unity of thought. Certainly I am not
wishing even in the most distant way to suggest
that we should cease to preach from the Bible,
still less that we should become journalistically
topical, hanging our own bright little ideas on
the peg of contemporary goings-on. I grow
more and more convinced that only Biblical
preaching, preaching based on the continuous
study of the Bible with all the help that modern
scholarship can give, is the least likely to be, not
a trickle of water over desert stones, quickly
dried up, but a broad, enduring river which
reflects heaven and fertilises the fields.

Nevertheless it is folly not to face the difficulty
with which the Bible presents us, counting perhaps
on God to suspend all psychological laws and
perform a miracle just because we are using Holy
Scripture. One incidental difficulty is that
people are far more ignorant of the Bible than
we ministers, who use it every day, realise. We
are in danger of assuming far too much, making
scriptural references and allusions which to many
hearers, alas, must be quite unintelligible, or at
least so vaguely identified as to contribute
nothing. Thus I remember a sermon in which

H

the only illustration the preacher gave of the point he was making was a reference to Hannah presenting Samuel in the Temple. I suspect that not many gained light from the reference. But the major difficulty I am sure is the sheer remoteness of the Biblical world and the incapacity of most people to discover that it has any pungent or deep-going relevance to the present day. It is not that they are not ready to be interested in the Biblical world. They are. But then they are not unready to be interested in any reconstruction of the past, if it is competently done. But to become aware of the final reality of *your* world meeting you through an exposition of David's world or Paul's, or even Christ's, that is another matter. Nay, indeed, to have that world skilfully presented to you may provide you with another temporary *escape* from your own in which alone God can livingly encounter the soul. I am sure that an otherwise really good sermon has lost effectiveness because of an insufficient realisation of this. I have so often heard sermons which have provided a competent and interesting analysis of, say, Elijah's or David's mental processes at certain crises of their life, or of those of the disciples or Paul, but have made no attempt, save perhaps in a perfunctory sentence or two, to confront *me*, the insurance clerk, or the shorthand typist, with that same living God meeting me in the here and the now of an existence which seems on the whole rather drab, because so familiar, in comparison with that world of long-ago.

The very desire of the preacher to evoke the past in a picturesque and interesting way—to hold his hearer's attention—may prove his undoing. The scene comes before the listener almost like a costume or period play, on the background of an advertisement of the P. and O. line—blue sky, white walls, robed figures and all the glamour of the mysterious East. How big the jump to the dirty flatness of the wet street on Monday morning, waiting for the 'bus by the mean little pub at the corner, the drab monotony, the long littleness, the mechanised fixity of factory work! Sometimes I have my doubts about the pictures of Biblical scenes with which we adorn our Sunday Schools. My doubts are not diminished by the reflexion that any other sort of picture would hardly do. We could not picture Christ in modern dress. But that illustrates our difficulty once again. The Bible *is* oriental, our world is not.

Perhaps I am exaggerating the difficulty in the attempt to make clear what I am after. But of its actuality I am certain, and I am equally certain that many preachers do not realise sufficiently that it is there. The difficulty is made greater by the setting in which we are given the task of preaching from these oriental books and scenes. The building itself suggests withdrawal from the everyday places and habits of our life—the arches and pillars, the stained-glass with saints in long robes and halos, the vestments, sometimes the solemn and unnatural tones of the preacher. Oh! that unnatural, pulpit voice which some ministers assume as soon as they enter the pulpit, as though their task were not difficult enough, as it is, to convey the relevance to everyday things of what they say. Why do they do it, why has nobody taken them to task for doing it? Is it because they confuse mere solemnity with seriousness and reverence? May I pause here to say a word about this? It is assuredly not unimportant.

The difference between mere solemnity and true seriousness and reverence is difficult to state, but easy enough to recognise in practice. The extreme expression of mere solemnity is, I always think, to be discerned in the participants in ecclesiastical ritual, especially ecclesiastical processions. I do not say that it is necessarily bound up with ecclesiastical ritual, but only that, if it is present at all, it manifests itself there unmistakably. Solemnity as distinct from true reverence sits plainly enough on the faces of choir-boys, though there it is not inappropriate and is faintly amusing. But in the adult members of the procession it becomes faintly nauseating, even though you know they are good folk and by no means hypocrites. It is not I hope merely Presbyterian prejudice which makes one recoil, as once I did from a priest bringing up the rear of an ecclesiastical procession with hands projecting stiffly in the conventional attitude of prayer, thumbs crossed, the eyes as closed as the necessity of not rendering himself completely blind permitted. For indeed the same thing can be observed amongst ourselves in the pulpit manner and the pulpit voice.

It is not a question of hypocrisy, of not having true reverence in one's heart ; it is that at the moment one is being merely solemn and therefore unnatural. Indeed in some ways the more serious one is, the more one is likely to fall into this error. At bottom the cause of the trouble is the cause of all our troubles—the " beloved ego ", an undue awareness of ourselves and our office. We are sincerely aware of God and of His call and commission, but we are also, when we go into the pulpit, very conscious of ourselves being aware of God and of His call and commission. We are like those tiresome people who do genuinely admire the sunset, but when they speak of it, you know at once that, in addition, they admire themselves admiring the sunset ; who appreciate music, yet are never fully absorbed in it, but have some attention left over for themselves appreciating music. Ultimately the only cure, I suppose, is the grace of God, but it is perhaps some help to bethink ourselves of the urgent necessity for natural directness in our speech, if we are not to add to the difficulty of keeping our message and the hearer in living touch with the real world.

Kierkegaard has some powerful words on the way in which preaching and its whole manner and setting can fail to relate itself to the concrete situations of real life wherein God meets man. As they illustrate some of the other points I have tried to make, perhaps I may be allowed to quote at some length :

" How quiet everything is in the house of God, what a sense of security. He who enters it feels as if by a single step he had arrived at a remote place, endlessly far away from all noise and outcry and vociferation, from the horrors of existence, from the storms of life, from the spectacle of dreadful events or from the sickly expectation of them . . . how comforting, how inviting—ah, and how much danger in this security ! Wherefore it is verily true that really it is only God in heaven who in the actuality of life can preach to men with effect ; for he has circumstances, has fates, has consternation in his power. And circumstances—and when ' thou ' art in them, when they enclose ' thee ' as the party properly concerned—yea, their eloquence is piercing and awakening.

That thou hast experienced too. In case thou wast the sick man who at the hour of midnight lay sleepless upon the sick-bed, or in case thou wast merely the one that sat at the midnight hour beside the sick man's couch of pain and with alarming distinctness counted every tick of the clock and every sigh of the sick man, but without finding relief in the uniformity or in the mechanical exercise of counting—if then thou didst hear that pious song, ' It was upon the midnight hour our Saviour he was born : ' dost thou believe that all orators put together would be able to produce this effect ? And why not ? Because the sick-bed and the hour preach more mightily than all orators, and understand this secret of speaking to thee in such a fashion that thou dost get an apprehension that it is thou, precisely ' thou ', not him that sits beside thee, not him out there, but precisely ' thou ' that art spoken to, thou who dost feel thyself alone, alone in the whole world, alone at the midnight hour beside the sick-bed. Or in case a man lies *in extremis* and fairly and honestly they have not concealed from him that which people desire to conceal from the dying man, the thing most important for him to know, that it is all over—dost thou not believe that the simple comforting word of the most commonplace man will produce an entirely different effect than is produced by all the most famous orators upon him who, sound and healthy . . . sits secure in the gorgeous church and hears . . . and perhaps criticizes the address. And why will that simple word produce an entirely different effect ? Because death knows how to make itself understood by the man to whom it applies, knows how to make thee understand that it is ' thou ', that thou art the individual in question, that it is not anybody else, not thy neighbour or thine opposite neighbour, or another man here in the town, but it is thou who art to die.

So it is in the actuality of life when it is God that preaches by means of circumstances to awaken. But in the house of God, in the splendid house of God, when the parson preaches . . . to tranquillise ! . . . So [men] sit perfectly secure in the house of God, becoming more and more fastidious in their desire for the trumpery of eloquence, because they well know that no orator has the power which providence has to lay hold of a man, to cast him off into the power of circumstance, to let the desperation and trials and alarms of it preach seriously to him for awakening." [1]

Kierkegaard, in his own sombre way, has put our difficulty : God comes in the actualities of life and we who preach must therefore at all costs keep contact with those concrete actualities ; yet how hard the task, how great the cost ! The Bible from which we preach, if we are not careful, and the whole ecclesiastical setting of worship, and even our pulpit manner and voice " remotises ", if I may coin a word, the hearer from what Kierkegaard calls the " power of circumstance ".

As to how the difficulty may be overcome I am afraid I have little counsel to offer, beyond what I have already said, namely that we must be constantly reminding ourselves of it and must prepare what we have to say with the deliberate intention and effort to overcome it. I have sometimes found it a help to write with a definite person in a definite situation before my mind's

[1] *Christian Discourses*, (Eng. Tr.), pp. 171f, one sentence transposed in the last paragraph.

eye, putting to myself such questions as these, How would this sound to him? would he understand it? would it seem any other than an airy and irrelevant abstraction? and so on. Years ago in the psychological laboratory in Cambridge we used to stage imaginary crimes and then try to detect the culprit from among a number of suspects by a prolonged application of association tests. A list of words was read out and each suspect had to give the first word that came into his mind as each was given; the time of the reaction was noted. In the list were one or two key words connected with the crime. By studying the reaction words and the times we never failed very quickly to detect the culprit, except in one instance. This culprit came into the examination deliberately filling his mind, as he told us afterwards, with a picture as remote from the crime as he could make it. He kept his thoughts fixed on a country farmyard scene. The result was that all his association words tended to be in terms of that scene, and it was only because he grew tired of the effort of attention involved that we got him in the end.

I apologise for the illustration, but it does at least make clear the way in which the mind can control its processes by a little technique and a little effort. If you write a sermon, for example, on the problem of suffering, I guarantee that the result will be very different if you write with your mind fixed on someone in a hospital bed rather than with your mind filled with what was said in a class-room theological lecture, though the essential truth of the latter may be what you really want to convey. At the same time it is necessary to be careful with your illustrations. Some preachers in their endeavour to escape from abstractness and to be concrete seem to think that any illustration is better than none at all. It is not. An illustration can make the message as unreal and remote as an abstract generalisation, indeed more so, for the very attempt at concreteness accentuates the failure to achieve it in a convincing way. Stories that have the least tincture of saccharine or sentimentality in them, or which in the least degree raise the question in the hearer's mind whether they could really have happened, should be omitted, even at the cost of having no illustration at all.

But perhaps even greater than all these difficulties is the one that was particularly emphasised by the Oxford Conference on Church, Community and State. It is the difficulty that the Church today is woefully out of touch with vast areas of the common life of the people. The result is we are before we even begin to preach in a somewhat abstracted and isolated position needing a special effort to overcome it. The Church is not wholly, or even perhaps mainly, to blame for this, which only makes the difficulty greater, for what we are not responsible for it is not easy to remedy.

There are two factors in this situation.

The first is the secularisation of all our life which has over a long period of years gradually taken place. The grand mediæval conception of the common life as a *corpus christianum*, which though it remained largely an ideal did attain a recognisable degree of realisation, has become, both in people's minds and in the actual conduct of the community's life, increasingly meaningless and irrelevant. Large spheres of the common life, such as schools, universities and hospitals, in which the Church was once pioneer and controller, have been taken over by the community. The great tasks of education, science, business, culture, go on with a momentum and purpose of their own, and not only is there no reference to the Church, but such a reference would now be regarded as a disturbance and an intrusion. In the big housing estates set up by municipal authorities it often happens that no provision is made for a church. Yet provision is made for community centres in which recreational, cultural and other common activities can be pursued on a secular basis. In the parish church in Kinghorn in Fife there hangs from the ceiling in one of the transepts—somewhat incongruously as it seems to us modern worshippers—the model of a ship. It marks what used to be called the " sailors' aisle ", the place where the sailors sat under the unmistakable emblem of their craft. Today it is but a relic of the past, and that it is a relic marks the change which has taken place and which we have in mind. Today people, even people in the churches themselves, think of religion, not as that which is relevant to, and informs, all activities, but as just one activity among others for those who happen to be inclined that way, like folk-dancing. It is something apart. The whole business of religion begins and ends in a situation of abstraction from the things that actually fill men's lives.

The other factor is this : The life of any man or woman is shaped by two great sets of conditions or influences. The one set of conditions has to do with the unchanging, universal needs of individual human life—human life, one might say, as such. You cannot be a human being at all without having just those needs. Any man, of any race, in any age, in any civilisation, at any stage of development feels, or is liable to feel, or can be brought to feel, these needs and to crave some sort of satisfaction for them, just because he is a man. Whoever he is, he has to face sooner or later, in one form or another, the facts of death, bereavement, disease and pain, frustration and disappointment of ambition and desire, the struggles and insecurities of making a living, the strains and tensions of personal relationships, the perplexities of conscience, the persistent pull and downdrag of evil in his own soul.

The other set of factors has to do with the external setting of his life. I mean the social environment and context of his existence, including in that both the framework of social, economic and industrial arrangements which so largely determine his existence, and those invisible influences which are soaking into him all the time and of which he is hardly aware, what we call vaguely the " spirit of the times." Obviously this external setting is not the same all the time. It differs from century to century, generation to generation, nation to nation. The first set of factors has a permanence and a universality which the second lacks. The former abide, the latter change, though always they are in interplay with one another. Men have always died, always suffered bereavement, always had ill-nesses, always had bad consciences, always needed personal forgiveness ; but they have not always lived under, say, industrial capitalism.

Now the situation in relation to the Church's message seems to be this. On the other hand, men are today overwhelmingly conscious of the second set of factors, conscious perhaps as they have never been before. They are still subject to the universal permanent needs of human life, of course, but these largely " come at " them through the social and industrial system of which they are a part, and which, they feel, bitterly aggravates them. As Dr. Oldham has said : " There is a relatively small number of privileged persons, including those who have private means and many clergy and teachers, who have consider-able freedom to direct their own lives. But for the vast majority who are directly engaged in economic activities, most of their acts and nearly all the consequences of their acts are outside their conscious control. Society has become inhuman, and most of its members cannot live, as God meant them to live, as responsible persons serving one another in a genuine community." [1] This on the one hand.

On the other hand, the Church in the past has

[1] *Christian News-Letter*, No. 57, Supplement.

on the whole concentrated on, specialised in, so to say, the application of its message to the first set of factors—the permanent and universal needs and troubles of individual men and women whatever their situation. It has had little or nothing to say about the second set, which, as we have said, is more and more filling the horizon of the masses. The result is that the gospel to multitudes seems, in a way that many would find difficult to put into terms, unreal, remote from the basic and absorbing problems of their life. The fact is men today are not asking primarily, or mainly, " What must *I* do to be saved? what comfort and strength and light are there for me in bereavement and disappointment and personal failure? " They are asking that, they have always asked it and always will ; these needs, I repeat, are permanent and universal, and we have a grand gospel for them. But they are primarily asking, " what must *we* do to be saved? " The dominant problem today is felt to be the problem of community. It is no good shutting our eyes to that fact, or wishing it were otherwise. If we believe in providence, the God of history, at all, we may well believe that God Himself has ordained that this shall be our main problem in these days, and if we in the churches run away from it, make no attempt at whatever cost to discover and declare the gospel's application to it, we shall be running away from God.[1]

For these two reasons then the Church finds itself in a situation of abstraction or remoteness from the common life of men, first the destruction of the *corpus christianum*, and second the dominance over people's lives of vast and complex community problems to which the Church has hardly as yet given its mind. The point for us as preachers is that this, if it be true, considerably intensifies the problem of relevant concreteness, a problem of the utmost importance if it be also true, as we have maintained, that God comes to men primarily through the situations of their daily life.

If you ask me how these difficulties may be overcome I am afraid I have very little to say. But I do not think that can properly be held against me, for the problem of the Church's remoteness, though it conditions our preaching and its effectiveness, is too deep and complex for the preacher as such to be charged with the responsibility of solving it. The responsibility is upon the whole Christian Church. Concerning

[1] Of course, there has always been a " problem of community " and thoughtful minds have pondered it from Plato onwards. What distinguishes our time is the magnitude of the problem, the impossibility of escaping it, or postponing it, its " totalitarian " quality so that it touches every aspect of our life, and, above all, the extent to which the masses are explicitly aware that it is *their* problem.

the Church's separation from the common life I can only refer you, and through you, the congregations to which you will minister, to the report of the Oxford Conference on the matter and the practical suggestions there made.[1] As for wider, social questions, it is certainly not the business of the preacher to make detailed suggestions in his sermons, for the solution of industrial, economic and political problems. That would require expert knowledge which he has not got, and in any case his prime task is to preach the Gospel. But I am convinced that a preacher ought to be continuously aware of the situation I have described, and that, if he is aware of it, it will affect the content and direction of his message in a way that will in some degree absolve it from the charge of remoteness and irrelevance to the actual stuff of history as men are living it, and fashioning it, and being fashioned by it, today. Certainly he ought to be continually laying these matters on the conscience of his people, particularly such as have more knowledge and experience to pronounce upon them, and more immediate power to do something about them.

[1] See *The Churches Survey their Task* Allen and Unwin Ltd., pp. 67, 188.

V

THE MESSAGE AND THE CONTEMPORARY MIND

IN this concluding lecture I propose to develop further what I said at the end of the last.

Our gospel is an unchanging gospel, obviously ; but the way in which we present it, and the things in it which need to be proclaimed, or re-proclaimed, with special emphasis and clarity, are determined by the situation, the mental and spiritual situation particularly, of those to whom we speak. The spirit of the times is a very real, if intangible, thing, and it always has something of the pressure and challenge of God in it. Eternal as the gospel is, there must be some translation of it into the present tense, some welding, to change the metaphor, of a hard, sharp point of thrusting relevancy on to the shaft of it, or to use a somewhat worn but useful simile, we must get on to the right wavelength, if we are to be heard. Otherwise we shall contrive to give to men the impression, which as I said last time they now, I fear, so largely have, that religion in general, and the Christian religion in particular, is just one activity of life, among many others, which some queer people pursue, who happen to have a taste that way.

Let us begin with the distinction which we have made between the two great sets of factors which condition men's lives, the first set comprising the universal, unchanging needs of individual men and women, so to speak, as such, the second comprising the external framework, or context, of their lives in social, industrial, political conditions, which are not permanent and universal but change from age to age, nation to nation, class to class.

It is clear that these sets of factors, though they are always distinguishable and in a way independent, for the one set is permanent and the other changing, are not in fact separable from one another. The unchanging, universal needs of our common humanity " hit " us all, but the way in which they " hit " us depends on our situation, on the external setting of our lives and what is going on in it. For example, the crashing in of death upon our life, rending and tearing the delicate fabric of our personal relationships, may happen to all of us at any time, as it certainly will at some time. But today, because of modern war, it has become an immediate threat to countless people irrespective of age or condition or sex. Man is born to trouble as the sparks fly upward, says the Scripture writer. It is our special destiny today to live in a context of history when the sparks have become a veritable furnace of flame.

Now it is the relative independence and yet close interrelation of these two sets of factors which set us, as it seems to me, our special problem in bringing the message of the gospel to our day and generation. We have to keep these two factors in balance and unity with one another, and very particularly we have to be aware of, and not forget, the second. When I say it is our special problem, I mean that it is a bigger problem for us now than at some other times, because the second set of factors is today so obsessive and so dominant in men's minds.

On the one hand we must hold to it strongly that the gospel is a gospel of succour and challenge to the individual soul, as we have more than once insisted throughout these lectures. It is God's word to man as man whatever his situation, whatever the external setting of his life. We must ask, and expect in the name of Christ the response of, decision and trust and obedience in the individual, who must in the end settle the matter in the private places of his own heart.

Yet on the other hand it is most important to realise that it is really hard for the modern man to listen to a message which is conceived in narrow terms of his own individual salvation and worthy living. This is a point where emphatically the way in which the private, personal, universal human needs of men and women are felt is profoundly influenced by the external setting and framework of the time, and more particularly by what we call the spirit of the time. A message and a challenge to them as individuals—and it cannot be repeated too often, it must be to them as individuals—is out of focus, on the wrong wavelength, if it be not conceived in terms of something larger than the individual, in terms, that is to say, of the problems of community life. That this is so is indicated by the fact that the evangelistic meeting of the type with which we were once familiar now cuts so very little ice. We are absolutely at one, or at least I hope we are, with the evangelistic enterprises of the end and turn of last century in the insistence on the necessity of individual salvation and individual decision. I hope there is something in us corresponding to, nay identical with, the " passion for souls " of Moody and Sankey or Torrey and Alexander. Nevertheless it is true to say that their methods effect little today.

It is no good mincing matters on this point. The modern man, even the Christian man, will not go near a gospel meeting of the traditional type. It is foolish to attribute this to the wickedness and indifference of the present generation. That is too easy. We have got to understand it. That such an easy explanation is false is indicated by the fact that many who will not go near a gospel meeting of the older " what must I do to be saved " type will come to hear, and will respond to, a presentation of the gospel which they feel will offer them an interpretation of the confusion and perplexity and heartbreak of human history and human society as a whole, not however excluding from that their own quite private and personal perplexities and heartbreaks. The gospel has got to have an unmistakable cosmic note in it, a note of community How could it be otherwise ? As I have put it elsewhere, the modern man cannot help thinking in these wider terms. He opens his newspaper and reads the world. He goes to the pictures and sees the world. He listens to the radio and hears the world. At the present moment his whole personal destiny is caught up like a piece of driftwood in a chaos of waters where two great world-seas meet. I do not know how far one may correctly argue from the undergraduates of a university to the general run of men—I suspect far more correctly than some might be inclined to think—but it is a fact that in neither Oxford nor Cambridge can you bring undergraduates together in any numbers for anything that they have reason to suspect will be an evangelistic meeting of the old type. But announce a series of expositions of Christian doctrine, making plain that you wish to point its relevance to this modern scene, and you can promise yourself, as has been proved by experience in both places, four or five hundred people throughout many weeks.

This then is our dilemma and problem today. We cannot, we must not, lose the individual note. It is absolutely basic to our whole Christian outlook and in particular to our work as preachers. We cannot preach except to the individual. But also we must so conceive our message that it is not merely, or even perhaps in its first emphasis and impact, individual. The two things must be held together. But it is far from easy to hold them together. They always tend to fly apart. One minor difficulty is the cleavage which is apt to arise between the older and the younger generation, particularly of ministers. The older generation finds it difficult to think in any other terms than those of the older evangelism, and they suspect, quite understandably and even in some degree with justification, that the emphasis on the wider reach of the message is but a substitution for the Christian gospel, in all its awful and unbelievable challenge and succour to the human spirit, of some thin wash of a social gospel. They do not see that it may rather be a question of grasping in fuller measure, at one of God's crisis points in history, the height, depth, length and breadth of that gospel, its everlasting and inexhaustible relevance to any and every stage of human history, for indeed it is about the centre of all history, Jesus Christ our Lord. On the other hand, the younger generation of ministers are apt to have an uneasy sense that the older type of evangelism is now out of place and ineffective—thus no doubt revealing that they are themselves the product of their time; nor are they any the worse for that, for what is of the spirit of the times is always, as we have said, in some measure of the providence of God. But they are apt to overlook, and in a measure to fail to share, the real concern and love for ordinary, individual men and women which lay behind what was called the passion for souls.

Now as some small help in this difficult task, I propose in the time left to me to try to draw out very briefly some of the main elements in the sense of need which the modern man or woman feels, as he is played upon by the specifically modern and contemporary setting and context of his life. I make no claim to be exhaustive in this analysis ; no doubt there are other and more important things that I have overlooked ; for, indeed, which even of the wisest heads amongst us could hope to read accurately the signs of such times as these ? I find the contemporary mood in this country extremely baffling. Yet if we are to serve the present age, we must try to understand it, and if we are to try to understand it we have no option but to generalise, however risky it may be and however much it may end in an unprofitable setting of one opinion against another. I can only report to you some of the things that have struck me and which, if they be true, are certainly relevant to our presentation of the Christian message.

The needs which I shall mention were I believe deep in the modern mind before this war began. Since the war began, in this country at any rate, they are being temporarily masked and partially satisfied in and through the war enterprise itself, yet at the same time deepened and strengthened. They are being temporarily masked and partially satisfied by the necessity of getting on with the job, and by the sense of exaltation and significance which come through the threat of danger, the excitement of national feelings, the awareness of having a part to play. But they are also being strengthened and deepened by the manifest horror and futility and irrational destructiveness of the war method itself, by the latent sense that the life which the war now temporarily fills will be left, when it is all over, emptier than ever. The situation is somewhat like that of the drug-taker, who satisfies his craving for the moment at the cost of making it more clamant later on.

This is at once the danger and the opportunity which confronts us. I believe that unless these needs can find their right satisfaction in religion, the result of their temporary masking and partial satisfaction in the war will be, when the war is over, a frightful intensification of them with unpredictable consequences. On the other hand, I believe that people are conscious as never before that they must find a right satisfaction for them in religion, or life will never be worth

living again. People are feeling through the
war enterprise how grand life can be when there
is something worth working and dying for, and
yet at the same time and for the same reason
they are haunted by a fear that perhaps there is
nothing finally worth living and dying for. In
the very process of being carried over the abyss
on a great enterprise they are the better able to
look right into it. There never was a greater
opportunity, therefore, for the Christian message,
if we can only present it relevantly, concretely,
and with power. If these remarks can contribute
only a little to that end, they will be justified.
At the very least they may deepen within you
the realisation of the superlative importance of
your work as preachers and teachers appointed,
in the mysterious providence of God, to serve
this tremendous present age.

First, there is that of which I have just
spoken in general terms. I believe that one of
the most tragic features of the spiritual climate of
our time during the past decade or so has been,
and still is, a certain underlying, depressed,
hollow sense of the futility and meaninglessness
of human existence. That is not the sort of
statement which one can prove. You move
about amongst people, hear them talk and talk
with them, read newspapers and books, observe

the subtle and recurrent moods of your own spirit, and then when it is pointed out to you, if indeed you have not already pointed it out to yourself, you know it is true. This civilisation of ours seems to have lost heart. As Gilbert Murray said of an earlier age, there is a certain failure of nerve. At the moment, as I have said, there is in the activity of war a temporary masking and repressing of this ; yet at the same time there is, or there will be, as is usual with repressions, an intensification of it.

What lies behind this loss of nerve and heart, this sense of futility ? If we reply that it is due to the loss of the sense of God, that might appear to be just the sort of glib diagnosis of the world's ills that religious people are so prone to give. Yet it is the truth, beyond question. The dimension of the eternal in things moral and spiritual, is like the third dimension in things physical. It is the third dimension which gives to the landscape a solid and satisfying quality of " realness ", as it is the absence of it which gives an air of unreality to, say, the back-cloth of the stage. So it is with the dimension of the eternal. Without it the whole picture of life becomes in time to the human spirit flat, unreal, futile.

We may put it another way. During the last war a name was coined by French doctors for a disease which made its appearance in prison camps. They called it " barbed-wire sickness ". One of its symptoms was an appalling sense of the futility and meaninglessness of existence. No matter what camp activities were organised, or with what vigour they were prosecuted, nothing could quite banish from the mind the awareness of the barbed-wire enclosure, the isolation from any task which might have real and lasting significance. So it is with the human spirit today. It has barbed-wire sickness. The source of it is the loss of the perspective, the dimension of the eternal. Life is closed in on itself. Chesterton has pointed out [1] that when men are doing the things in life they feel to be really worth doing they always talk the language of eternity. On the other hand, if they cannot talk the language of eternity, they cannot be permanently and fully convinced that anything, however temporarily exciting and interesting, is really worth doing. When Leonidas called on the Spartans to die at Thermopylæ he did not say to them " I am inclined to think, and doubtless on consideration you will agree with me, that on the whole Spartan civilisation is preferable to

[1] *The Uses of Adversity*, p. 120.

Persian." He cried, "Sparta *for ever*". Lovers vow themselves to one another for ever. The Englishman cries "There'll always be an England". Even Hitler has to speak of a Reich that shall last a thousand years.

Second, I suspect that a very high proportion of individuals today are oppressed by a sense of their own personal insignificance.

I mean by this something different from the sense of the general meaninglessness and futility of things of which I have just spoken, though it is of course not unrelated to it. I have in mind something much more intimate, much more of the stuff of everyday relationships. Perhaps I should get nearest to what I have in mind if I were to say, using the current jargon, that a very high proportion of ordinary folk have something in the nature of an inferiority complex. No one who observes human behaviour all about him from day to day, including his own, with an understanding eye, can fail to note this. Sooner or later, and usually sooner than later, you catch almost anyone with whom you have to deal defending, asserting, his own importance. The amount of touchiness, quickness to take offence, that is to be met with in human relationships is pathetic, and is I believe of the greatest significance in the understanding of the contemporary situation. People are fighting all the time against a sense of personal insignificance. This is the result in part of the mass organisation of modern society, and the widespread depersonalisation of human relationships in the mechanised large-scale industry of today. It is part of the hunger of the human spirit for love, or, if you like, for justice, which is one aspect of love, in the midst of the profoundly loveless and unjust system in which they find themselves caught up. For only love can give a man a right sense of significance, as I think modern psychology is coming to see. But it is also the result of a whole system of social values and honours, class distinction, monetary rewards, which excite the desire of all, but in the nature of things can satisfy only a few. And few having the incentive or capacity to break away from the constant pressure of accepted systems of values, most people carry with them a continuous sense of incapacity, frustration, insignificance and inferiority. The result is that they try to recover the sense of significance in more or less perverted ways.

This is not to exaggerate a relatively unimportant thing. Galsworthy has said somewhere that the strongest motives determining human behaviour are not those which spring from the instincts and impulses which men share with the brutes, such as sex or hunger, but those which spring from the desire to " save face ". There is truth in this. Not only do inferiority feelings create unhealthy and unhappy personal relationships in more private matters, but also they have much to do with exaggerated national-istic feelings and with such a baffling phenomenon as anti-semitism. The inferior man enlarges his own ego to more satisfactory dimensions by identifying it with the nation, or, within the nation, by insisting that there is one class of person to whom he is always and absolutely superior, namely the outcast. It is surely not without significance that the most exaggerated nationalism and the most frightful anti-semitism of modern times have arisen in a country where there was more inferiority feeling concentrated in every square mile than anywhere else.[1]

Third, there is in men and women today a yearning for security.

Now, of course, men have always yearned for security. There is nothing new in that. Also it may be questioned whether such a craving is a right craving, whether there is not a finer instinct in man which is also manifesting itself today, namely the craving for adventure. But what I have in mind cannot be so lightly dis-

[1] Cf. K. Mannheim, *Man and Society*, p. 136.

missed.   Man does hunger for risk and adventure, and he grows weary of the principle of " safety first ".   But that hunger, if it is to find and bring satisfaction, requires a context of stable circumstance on which some reliance can be put. There is adventure in being at sea in a seaworthy boat with a storm rising ; there is no adventure in being at sea in such circumstances in a sieve. It is the difference between what has been called incidental and relative insecurity on the one hand and radical and fundamental insecurity on the other, between, let us say, burst pipes and an earthquake.   Those who have been in an earthquake tell of the ghastliness of the feeling of radical, all-inclusive insecurity.

It is something akin to the latter which is present in many people's minds today, though they could not put it into terms.   It is the feeling that the whole framework of life is rocking and shifting, that the broad, inclusive stabilities, within which quite a lot of incidental insecurity might be coped with, are no longer there. When we are in a somewhat exalted mood we express this in some such phrase as " mankind has struck its tents and is on the march again ". On a less exalted plane we say " everything is in the melting-pot ".   On a still less exalted plane, and one that comes nearest to the uncom-

fortable sense of foreboding which underlies the
brave face we put on, we say " civilisation
seems to be collapsing and God alone knows
what will arise from the ruins ". In many this
finds expression in an almost agonised concern
for their children, and even, in some, in a refusal
to have children at all.

Fourth, and reinforcing this, there is to be
observed in men and women today a rather
shocked, and even frightened, awareness of the
power of what can only be called the forces of
evil and of unreason which are at work in
history.

It is superfluous to go into the reasons for this.
The last war gave a nasty shock to the confident
belief in the essential reasonableness and goodness,
subject no doubt to unfortunate lapses and
fluctuations, of human nature, and in the possibility of building within a measurable period of
years a human society not altogether unworthy
even to be dignified by the name of the kingdom
of God. But the belief still lingered on, at least
in this country, in the sense that it still dominated
the subconscious processes of people's minds,
even though in their conscious thoughts they were
aware of the lurid interrogation marks which
1914–18 had written in the skies. The confidence
in the League of Nations shows this. But all

that has happened since 1930 has, I think, shaken men's minds right down to the subconscious springs of feeling and belief. A veritable abyss has opened at their feet. They have looked in and the flames are scorching their faces. They see a pit of unreason and evil, and an unspeakable hell of suffering, in the heart of human affairs. And it all seems to provide shocking verification of what the psychologists have been saying for so long about the hidden, unconscious forces which shape men's behaviour in spite of their pride in themselves as rational beings. Nor does the modern man, just for that very reason, feel inclined to run away from these facts. The psychologists have evoked in him a new fear, the fear of " wish-thinking ".

Fifth, there is in the modern mind a feeling of need for an absolute for conduct.

Men feel themselves to be adrift in uncharted seas without any clear sense of an object, or any principle which enables them to choose between competing interests or goals. There does not seem to be any reason for choosing one way of life rather than another. There are no fixed co-ordinates of reference. But, it may be asked, why should that worry anybody? Why not drift, do what you feel inclined to do? Drifting is not unpleasant. The answer is connected with the fundamental nature and needs of personality. It is only when a man has discovered an absolute of some kind in the sphere of behaviour that he begins to be released from subservience to his world like that of an animal, and becomes a person. Implicit in an absolute for conduct there is, as Oman has insisted, the conquest of all fear and the beginning of all mastery of one's world. And since man by the essential constitution of his being is meant to be a person, drifting in the end becomes intolerable, and, in a world radically insecure as this is today, a nightmare. This connects with what was said earlier about there being no real comfort for man apart from some claim or demand made upon him.

There is another reason why men today are hungry for an absolute for conduct. It is that on the whole they are more interested in " doing " than in " theorising and explaining ". That is partly the result of the pressure of events ; when the house is on fire or an earthquake shakes it, you do not go into the theory of heat or of geological faults ; you want to be told what to do. But it is also the result of a compensatory reaction against the exaggerated intellectualism which has for so long ruled in education and culture.

The supreme illustration of all this is, of course, the emergence of dictators and the leadership-principle. In the leader, wielding unquestioned authority, men find the hunger for an absolute for conduct and for active participation in significant events satisfied. Moreover the absolute has a personal form. No doubt all this is very perverted and ill-balanced, and in its satisfying of men's needs it contrives also to degrade and devaluate them ; but that it can hold men in the very process of degrading and devaluating them shows that deep and legitimate and unalterable necessitities of human life are involved.

There are, then, these five deep, persuasive needs and disquietudes manifesting themselves in greater or less degree in the mood and temper of our contemporaries.

Now, as I contemplate them, I do continually recover the sense of the direct, practical relevance of the Christian message to them. The Christian message fits these needs—all of them, not one or two at the expense of others, but all of them together. In these days when all men's activities and thoughts are concentrated on the immediate, crude, sheerly physical necessities of waging war, I have, I confess, often to put myself through a process of thought to recover the sense of the relevance of my work as a preacher and a theologian, or even the sense of the relevance of what is incomparably greater than one such insignificant person, the Christian Church itself. The process of thought is to remind oneself of those things, among others, of which we have been speaking. If it is possible at all to grasp, and make generalisations about, what is going on in the mind of our contemporaries, then we can confidently affirm that these disquietudes are not unrelated to the dissolving away from the minds of men, right down to the subconscious levels, of the Christian interpretation of life, and what is required therefore, above all things else, is that that interpretation should be restored. There are not lacking signs that many are themselves beginning to be aware of this. They are sensing, however dimly, that what they lack is a religious basis for life, and, confronted with shocking clarity by the sort of thing that can rush in and fill the gap, there is at least a disposition to turn to a specifically Christian basis if they can only understand it and see its relevance. I would wish to avoid exaggeration here. The amount of sheer paganism which is all about us is appallingly great. On the other hand it would be foolish not to discern the day of opportunity which is being given us by the heart-shaking events of these times.

One thing is clear—our preaching has got to be strongly doctrinal, not in the manner of the theological lecture room, but in such wise that doctrine and life are seen to be inseparably bound up together. It has got to *teach* the Christian interpretation of life in all its fulness. Yet it has to do this, without any loss of that concreteness, that thrusting relevance, that direct I–thou relationship, of which we have spoken so much.

Let me, then, in conclusion try to indicate, with a briefness which I fear may lay me open to the charge of that very abstractness which has been condemned, the relation of the great Christian doctrines to the needs of men which have been set forth.

First, the affirmation which Christianity makes of a divine purpose in history which a man is called to serve here and now, and yet which transcends history in its final consummation— so that our right to believe in it and commit ourselves to it is not affected by any disaster or darkness of this world whatsoever—guards the soul once and for all against barbed-wire sickness. It opens up within the heart of this passing world a vista of the eternal, yet not in such wise that this passing world is robbed of its significance and we are landed in that false otherworldliness which is a mere opiate, and, so far from allaying, in the end only serves to accentuate the sense of the futility of things. The eternal purpose is in history and we are called to serve it and have part in it ; history is significant for it. Yet, being eternal, it is not contained in history and is never to be construed merely in terms of what can be observed going on immediately around us.

Second, according to the Christian faith, this eternal purpose, though thus of cosmic and supra-cosmic scope, is a purpose of love, that is to say, it bestows the richest possible significance upon the individual person. One aspect of the relevance to the contemporary situation of this affirmation of the significance given to the individual because God's love rests upon him, has been so often pointed out that I need not dwell upon it. The appalling devaluation of the individual in our time is writ large across the totalitarian state, and it would be possible to find other examples nearer home. In the last resort the only effective defence against this kind of thing is the gospel of the love of God to individual men and women. But what I have more in mind is the relation of that gospel to the inner life of the individual himself.

Belief in the eternal purpose of God as an individualising love is an indispensable factor in any proper and permanent dealing with those feelings of inferiority and frustration with which so many of us are accursed and which poison the well of family life itself.   The only way in which that strange, paradoxical humility can be achieved, which is at once self-confident and without false superiority or inferiority feelings, is for a man to be daily confronted in the innermost places of his being with a reality which at one and the same time abases him and lifts him up. Furthermore the awareness of the eternal purpose of God meeting us, lighting upon us, in this world, yet transcending this world, begins a release from all those false values which hold us in thrall and so continually excite feelings of inferiority and frustration.   The relation of sound Christian teaching and belief to psychological health is close and deep, and has perhaps not yet been sufficiently explored.

Third, the Christian doctrine of providence, of the overshadowing and indwelling purpose and wisdom of God in history obviously relates itself to that distressing sense of radical insecurity, of the breaking up of foundations, which haunts the modern mind.   When the feeling of insecurity is so radical, it cannot be met by a glib, blandly optimistic affirmation about the future, nor by any construction, however clever, of blue-prints of a better world. It can only be met by something as radical, namely an ultimate declaration and decision of the soul about *God*. What is required is a final, almost naked, act of faith which cuts through, and makes superfluous and irrelevant, the arguments of philosophers which can never do more than make God a probable hypothesis, an act of faith which knows as in a supreme crisis that a man must either rest in God or go out finally into night. It is true that man's extremity is God's opportunity ; but it is also the devil's. Indeed it is only God's perhaps because it is the devil's ! I doubt sometimes whether any man can have a really strong and mature faith in God until he has looked into, and recoiled from, the ghastly abyss that life is without Him.

This leads to the fourth point, namely that the Christian doctrine of the love of God is not a glib and easy doctrine. There is at the heart and centre of it the Cross, and that disposes of the accusation of mere wish-thinking. The prime evidence of God's presence and action in history is not precariously sought in the good and pleasant things of life—the birds, the flowers, the sweet innocence of children—but in an event in which were operative the most evil impulses and deeds of men. Never was I more thankful than I now am that this is so, that the Christian message has at its heart the Cross, the doctrine of the divine love made manifest and winning its victory through such a horror of suffering and sin. Never before, certainly, was it more necessary for our preaching to centre in the Cross.

Fifth, in the call to loyal discipleship to Christ there is satisfaction for the deep, ineradicable need for a fixed point, an absolute, in the realm of conduct, the need which finds perverted satisfaction in the dictator-idea. Such perversion, with its degrading and shackling of the personality, is avoided because the doctrine of the leadership, the mastership, of Christ is inseparable from the doctrine of the Holy Spirit, Who takes of the things of Christ and shows them to all who seek to do His will, creating in the disciple that same mind that was in Him, without, however, asking him to be other than himself or to walk otherwise than by his own insight into the truth.

Yet, having said all this, I am conscious again of its inadequacy, true and important as I believe it to be. It all sounds so abstractly doctrinal, and the needs of men's hearts and lives, the needs of our civilisation, are so pressingly concrete. It is your task and mine as preachers and teachers to present this grand, deep gospel so that it ceases to be merely abstract and doctrinal and becomes thrustingly relevant to everyday affairs. It is a most difficult and responsible task, but, I repeat, we must not shirk it.

If we are to undertake it with any confidence at all, we must rest on the New Testament thought of what may be called the improbabilities of God, beginning with the most grotesque of all improbabilities, which is that a crucified man in an obscure land should be the Saviour and Judge of the world. " The first shall be last and the last first." " He hath pulled down the mighty from their seats and exalted them of low degree." " God hath chosen foolish things of the world to confound the wise ; and God hath chosen the weak things of the world to confound the things which are mighty." Among the foolish and weak things is surely our preaching. The foolishness of preaching ! No one should go into this ministry, least of all in these days, without an explicitly and tenaciously held faith in the over-shadowing providence and manifold wisdom of God, that providence and wisdom in relation to which a life, a deed, even a sermon, which from a worldly and natural point of view appears to be of no consequence at all, which indeed is so obscure that nobody of any importance notices it at the time and it will never be inscribed on the pages of secular history, can yet bear much fruit both in this world and in the world to come.

INDEX